Instructional Adaptation as an Equity Solution for the English Learners and Special Needs Students

*Practicing Educational Justice
in the Mainstream Classroom*

Jose W. Lalas
Margaret Solomon
University of Redlands

KENDALL/HUNT PUBLISHING COMPANY
4050 Westmark Drive   Dubuque, Iowa 52002

CONTENTS

PREFACE AND ACKNOWLEDGEMENTS

We have spent many hours discussing, arguing, debating, achieving consensus, and carefully researching the issues we are presenting in this book. It did not matter where we were or what we had in our hands—a yellow pad, a notebook, a piece of napkin, or even a yellow post-it, on the plane, at the airport, at the restaurant or cafeteria, in a faculty meeting—we wrote ideas, outlined and re-outlined topics, and transcribed our thoughts. Selecting a topic related to English language learners and special needs students proved natural to both of us because of our cultural and professional background experiences. We are both bilingual and multicultural, grew up in a different culture, and taught in U.S. public schools that seemed "foreign" to us because we were born, raised, and educated in two different countries outside the U.S. Both of us have an advanced degree in literacy and have taught reading and language arts, English as a second language, and special education in K-12 urban settings. We are very thankful of these blessed prior experiences that serve as a rich pool of resources for our thinking, disposition, and collaboration in writing this book.

We would like to thank those who inspired us to carry out our qualitative research and the writing of this book for pre-service and in-service teachers—and they are the English language learners and special needs students. Without these special students, this book would never have been. We also would like to thank our colleagues at the University of Redlands' School of Education for giving us the opportunities to dialogue with them and making us realize that they, too, are for providing equity, care, and educational justice to our marginalized diverse students in public schools.

We would like to extend our special appreciation to our pre-service teachers whose responses on the Teacher Performance Assessment tasks provided part of the data for the book. We would like to give our deep gratitude to our in-service teachers Theresa Palmer, Anita Villalpando and Valesca Dwyer who collaborated with us in planning for adaptation activities, implementing instructional adaptations in their classrooms, and providing the qualitative data for Chapter 3. We also would like to acknowledge the contribution of our colleague Dr. Gary Stiler in writing chapter 4. We want to thank Linda Tymchek for doing the initial editing of some of the chapters. We are very grateful to Michelle Bahr, the project coordinator for Kendall/Hunt Publishing Company, for giving us the opportunity to share our expertise. And finally, we owe so much to our spouses Linda Lalas and Poovelingam Solomon, and other family members who have always supported and inspired us to bring this book to fruition.

INTRODUCTION

Any preservice or inservice teacher faced yet with another book on second-language acquisition or working with special needs students deserves to raise a red flag of skepticism because of the abundance of published materials available and the amount of redundancy in these fields of study. However, our book is different because it is not only practical and theoretical, it is also grounded in the notion of **equity** and **educational justice** for the schooling of English language learners (ELLs) and special needs students (SNSs). This book is indeed a unique undertaking because it examines the needs of both these special groups of students and recommends practical classroom-based and equitable adaptation strategies to facilitate their learning of subject-matter content. In addition, the contents of this practical book should be refreshingly unique, for there is evidence of rigor, passion, ethic of caring, and advocacy for issues critical to enhancing the language, literacy, and academic development of ELLs and SNSs from a specific perspective of making the necessary instructional adaptations to facilitate success in mainstream classrooms. Both preservice and inservice teachers need to exhibit effectiveness in making adaptations for ELLs and SNSs to facilitate their access to academic content as well as develop their communication skills, dispositions, and habits of mind.

It has been a well-established fact that English learners are not performing well academically, and students with special needs are not thoroughly being served to reach their full potential compared to other students in schools. These are not surprising phenomena, given the objective difficulty of understanding academic content as well as social discourse in a language foreign to them, in the case of the ELL, or in an academic program that does not match the student's preparation, experience, and learning proficiency, in the case of the SNS. In addition, this dilemma in public schools is often associated with race, ethnicity, and poverty. Our main intent in writing this book is to develop teachers who can make subject-matter content comprehensible and academic success reachable for English learners and students with special needs despite their evident obstacles. We take special care in integrating theory, research, and best practice in our adaptation strategies and recommendations. We seriously examine the variety of inequities that exist in K–12 settings, their impact on academic achievement, and how "making adaptation" is an effective way of providing an equity solution for the education of the ELLs and SNSs and contributing to "narrowing the literacy gap" (Barone, 2006; Gunning, 2006).

While there have been attempts to legislate educational reforms to bring improved academic achievement for all learners, these efforts are generally inconsistent with research and best practice in the area of second-language learning and teaching. In the case of English learners in California, for example, Proposition 227 mandates that such students must be taught in English, assuming that 1 year of intensive English instruction would be enough to make ELLs proficient enough to function in mainstream classrooms. Although research in second-language learning says that 5 to 7 years are needed for ELLs to become proficient in the target language for academic purposes (Cummins, 1986), the program and instructional implications for this finding have not been considered at the policy level. In the case of the students with special needs, the continuing trend is for inclusion within the general education classroom in which teachers are supported as they, in turn, attempt to provide support for the education of students who have demonstrated learning disabilities such as perceptual dysfunction, attention and memory deficits, problems using oral or written language to learn, and many other special learning conditions. It has been reported that about 80% of students classified as learning disabled have a reading difficulty (Gunning, 2005).

There is a high expectation that aside from subject-knowledge competence, teaching methods coursework, field experience, and performance assessment, preservice and inservice teachers need to have the ability and disposition to work in high-poverty and hard-to-staff schools where many English language learners and special needs students attend. The common approach in meeting the academic needs of ELLs and SNSs in these schools is to expect teachers to make instructional adaptations to facilitate access to subject-matter content as a way of decreasing the achievement gap between mainstream students who are English speakers, on one hand, and the second-language learners and special needs students, on the other hand. It is indeed a top priority for teacher preparation programs to develop beginning teachers who are prepared and grounded on how to effectively instruct ELLs and SNSs in their mainstream classrooms using language, literacy, and academic content adaptation strategies.

We take the view that language, literacy, and academic content adaptation is a process of making information associated with academic disciplines accessible and understandable to English learners and special needs students. Academic content adaptation may include attempts to make learning comprehensible by using scaffolding techniques such as visuals, semantic maps, vocabulary knowledge practice, notetaking on key ideas from lectures, charts and tables, and research papers or book reports. Although the state's K–12 academic content standards specify the knowledge, skills, and strategies to be mastered by the end of the designated grade, there is no guarantee that students, especially the English learners and special needs students, build on these abilities toward higher-order critical thinking skills and deeper analysis and interaction with the text across content areas.

Instructional adaptation of academic content is imperative in facilitating the academic success of the ELLs and SNSs in mainstream classrooms. This could mean that teachers, in facilitating academic success, will focus on competencies that develop the "basic skills" as well as foster critical thinking and higher-order thinking skills in reading, such as summarizing, making connections, synthesizing, arguing with the text, determining the major and subordinate ideas, interpreting, evaluating, applying, and suspending information while searching for answers to self-generated questions.

Language, literacy, and academic content adaptation for ELLs and SNSs also means providing them with ample opportunities for reading and writing as means of thinking and gaining access to academic content while reinforcing their basic word recognition skills. Teachers need to engage students in language, literacy, and academic content activities for different purposes with attention to audience while learning, analyzing, summarizing, synthesizing, evaluating, and generating ideas, information, or arguments.

In addition, teachers need to engage ELLs and SNSs in oral discourse for full participation in intellectual discussion and acquisition of skills necessary for effective academic literacy, such as understanding directions for assignments, listening while simultaneously taking notes, retaining information, and participating in small-group and whole-class discussions. Comprehensible speech is equally essential because engaging in intellectual discussions and debates, as well as self-advocacy and questioning, depend on clear speech and well-developed vocabulary.

Technology is important for language, literacy, and academic content adaptation for student success. This is because the nature of knowing and thinking has changed dramatically. Students do not learn facts but learn to find, evaluate, use, and communicate information in a variety of formats. To do so requires intellectual sharing, discussion, and critical reading, writing, and thinking. Preservice and inservice teachers need to serve as facilitators of the use of technology as a tool for making effective language, literacy, and academic content adaptation.

To cover all the aforementioned knowledge, skills, abilities, and dispositions related to language, literacy, and academic content adaptation, we divided this book into five major chapters. The first chapter presents the history and policy development of second-language instruction and educational effort to meet the demands of special needs students. The second chapter explains the nature and conceptual framework of adaptation, in which we attempt to link it to sociopolitical and sociocognitive dimensions and show its value as a tool for equity solutions for learning and teaching in the classroom. The third chapter is a research-based report that introduces the notion of teaching performance assessment (TPA), identifies aspects of "good teaching," and describes how beginning and experienced teachers make instructional adaptations for ELLs and SNSs in mainstream classrooms. It highlights specific categories and examples of adaptation approaches and strategies as tools for equity solutions. The fourth chapter consists of several literacy and technology "teaching tips" related to making language, literacy, and academic content adaptation effective across disciplines. It suggests many practical literacy and technology support activities and strategies that are highly relevant and appropriate for ELLs and SNSs. The final chapter is a reflection of our optimism and summarizes the essential ingredients for making and sustaining instructional adaptations a successful vehicle for providing equitable solutions to the challenges of the English language learners and special needs students in the classroom.

Jose W. Lalas
Margaret Solomon
August 2006

REFERENCES

Barone, D. (2006). *Narrowing the gap: What works in high-poverty schools?* New York: The Guilford Press.

Cummins, J. (1986). Empowering minority students: A framework for intervention. *Harvard Education Review, 15,* 18–36.

Gunning, T (2005). *Creating literacy instruction for all students.* Boston, MA: Pearson Education Inc.

Gunning, T. (2006). *Closing the literacy gap.* Boston, MA: Pearson Education Inc.

Serving the English Language Learners and Special Needs Students in the Mainstream Classroom

Ms. Graves is a newly credentialed teacher who is a broad minded and conscientious professional. She has been advised and alerted that her California classroom will have a diverse student body that will include English language learners (ELLs) who have not achieved grade-level English proficiency and special needs students (SNSs) who have been recently mainstreamed. She gained excellent content knowledge in science while pursuing her undergraduate degree and acquired various subject-matter teaching methods in the teacher credential program. Yet this highly motivated science teacher faces the challenge of planning her instruction to meet the needs of all learners, including the English language and special needs learners whose instructional demands are very different from each other. As she considers the complexity of her teaching assignment she wonders what she must do to excel in her profession.

Undoubtedly, Ms. Graves experiences great frustrations when English learners lacking academic English language proficiency do not perform the learning tasks according to her expectations. There are four to five ELLs in each of her class periods, and her principal, Mr. Jones, who is a big supporter of "inclusion" for special education students, has allowed three of them in her fourth-period 11th-grade biology class. Two of them are high-functional students with learning disabilities (LD)—David and Corey—and the third is Johnny, who is autistic. This teacher strives daily to teach all students effectively but her ELLs and SNSs are not doing well in her classes. She is very much aggravated with the enormous responsibility put on her to teach these high-needs students who are unable to learn grade-level content materials. This example explains the intensity of the instructional dilemma experienced by many teachers in mainstream classrooms around the nation. The following illustration shows that challenge:

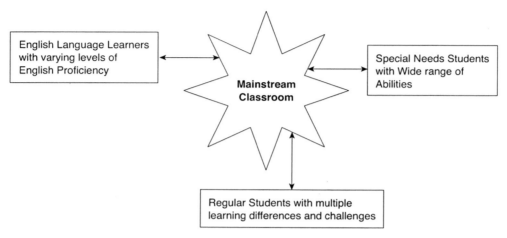

Dilemma in the mainstream classroom.

The recent data released on student achievement shows that the academic achievement of English language and special needs learners is only at the marginalized level. According to the Nation's Report Card released through the National Assessment of Educational Progress by the U.S. Department of Education (NAEP, 2005), there is a "paralysis" in the achievement of fourth- and eighth-grade ELLs and SNSs in the areas of reading and math. These two special groups' achievement scores show some progress in the longitudinal sense, but in comparison with the progress of the majority students the gap is still very wide and demonstrates a pattern of widening even further. For example, in the area of reading in grade 4, there is a very high discrepancy, with over 70% of ELLs achieving only at the below-basic level, while over 73% of first-language learners from the majority group are achieving at the proficient and advanced levels. Similarly, 79% of special needs learners in the fourth grade scored at the below-basic level in reading. The math results show similar trends. In grade 4, 46% of ELLs scored at the below-basic level in math, while only 17% of regular students functioned at the below-basic level. Similarly, of the special needs learners in fourth grade, 44% functioned at the below-basic level. This set of data clearly indicates that the steps taken to bring the ELLs and SNSs to mainstream classrooms have not changed the dismal picture of their academic achievement. The instruction of ELL is "caught in the cocoon," while the instruction of special needs learners in the mainstream is "paralyzed" with ineffective teaching and marginalization.

HOW DID THEY GET THERE?

The described dilemma in the mainstream classroom makes one raise the question, "What led to the integration of the English language and special needs learners into the mainstream classroom?" In order to understand how these students with special learning needs landed in mainstream classrooms we have to look at the history and evolution of progress related to second-language instruction and working with special needs learners. These two areas of educational interest have been greatly dependent on federal educational policies for funding and special provisions for developing instructional programs because they were considered on the pretext of bringing educational equity for all learners. That reasoning has been instrumental in bringing these learners into the mainstream classrooms. A historical review will show how educational reform efforts brought these two groups of students to the mainstream classroom with an accountability mandate currently demanding academic performance similar to all other learners.

HISTORICAL DEVELOPMENT OF SECOND-LANGUAGE INSTRUCTION IN THE UNITED STATES

Teaching English to students who speak other languages is not a new phenomenon in this country. Even during the colonial period when English was emerging as the main language of this new nation, people who spoke languages other than English had the freedom to learn and develop their first languages. Other languages were tolerated and allowed to exist. In the later years, there were periods when English exerted its importance over other languages, including those of the Native Americans. After World War I and World War II, more restrictions on German and Japanese language were made. However, in the 1960s, due to the influence of the civil rights movement, Congress passed the Bilingual Education Act (BEA) as part of the ESEA Act on January 2, 1968, which later became the Title VII bilingual education program. This federal mandate for bilingual education has gone through ups and downs in the past 38 years, and then was absorbed by No Child Left Behind (NCLB) law in 2002. In the progression of the policy on second-language instruction, the political and educational arenas have been daunted by two ideologies. The idea of "English only" supports the view that the speakers of languages other than English assimilate into the dominant culture and language by achieving proficiency in English. On the other hand, "English plus" supports the idea of attaining English proficiency through bilingual instruction and maintaining first-language proficiency as well. However, the federal law from its inception neither made it clear nor prescribed whether English only or English plus was preferred for ELLs. Although named the Bilingual Education law, this overall sweeping mandate did not endorse either bilingualism or English immersion and failed to answer the key question of whether second-language learners should maintain their first language as they learn English.

The BEA initially prescribed that educational opportunities should be extended to students who speak languages other than English and specified that meaningful instruction for English language learners should be provided. Senator Yarborough, the sponsor of this bill, made it clear to fellow lawmakers that "it is not the purpose of the bill to create pockets of different languages throughout the country . . . not to stamp out the mother tongue, and not to make their mother tongue the dominant language, but just to try to make those children fully literate in English" (Crawford, 1995, p. 40). The second-language educational policy mainly provided a small but significant change in practice for teaching linguistic minority students (Ovando & Collier, 1985). It did not come as a pedagogical response to the learning needs of English learners but as a political effort to funnel federal poverty funds to the Southwest region (Casanova, 1995) to children who did not speak English as their first language. It first listed three educational purposes: "1. Increase English language skills, 2. Maintain and perhaps increase mother-tongue skills, and 3. Support the cultural heritage of the student" (Leibowitz, 1980).

In essence, this law gave a jump start for developing instructional programs that would serve the needs of ELLs but did not provide a clear instructional answer to the question of how to teach English to ELLs, and it did not clarify whether biliteracy was a definite goal. That has resulted in many tensions and dilemmas in the arena of second-language instruction, which has been on a tumultuous course of development from its inception. The policy did not provide the necessary support for teaching English in the most effective way. Consequently, learning English for ELLs began as a scattered instruction in various parts of the country emerging as an instructional program that did not have a clear end goal; therefore, it never achieved its full maturity.

In addition, when the Bilingual Education Act (BEA) was reauthorized in 1974, amendments to the law emphasized the importance of mastery of English language skills as its main purpose. Although native language instruction was mentioned, the revised law of 1974 "provided more precise definition of the bilingual education program required in English and the child's native language to the extent needed for the child to make effective progress" (Alexander & Alexander, 1992, p. 274). Ironically, although the structure and operation of the BEA were expanded, the amendments to the law "barred federal support for two-way bilingual programs such as the successful Coral Way model" at Dade County in Florida (Lyons, 1995, p.3).

In the same year the landmark Supreme Court case *Lau vs. Nicholas* upheld the fact that there was no equality of treatment for the monolingual Chinese students enrolled in San Francisco Unified School District. It specified that providing the same textbooks, teachers, and curriculum to students who did not understand English was an unequal treatment; however, it did not mandate that first language be taught or used to teach English. The *Lau* decision fell short of that and listed remedies suggested by Title VI of the Civil Rights Act prescribing proper approaches, methods, and procedures for determining appropriate instructional methods and professional standards for teachers of language minority students.

When the next reauthorization cycle of the Bilingual Education Act came in 1978, research on bilingual education had accumulated findings that were generally supportive of bilingual educational programs (Casanova, 1995). As a result, the act was amended with new goals. It specified that native language would be used to enable the second-language learners to achieve competence in the English language and not primarily to maintain it. It also made sure that the Title VII program would be strictly transitional and no funds would be available for language maintenance. Later, during the Reagan administration, political opposition to bilingual education arose. The administration's view was well expressed in these words: "It is absolutely wrong and against American concepts to have a bilingual education program that is now openly, admittedly dedicated to preserving students' native language and never getting them adequate in English so they can go out into the job market" (*Democrat-Chronicle*, 1981, p. 2A).

When the time for reauthorization of Title VII arrived in 1984, the background work of the legislators and their courtship of Hispanic votes in the election propelled the bill quickly toward passage. In 1988, the BEA was reauthorized with some other changes when President

Reagan signed P.L. 100–297 into law on April 28, 1988. This bill allowed funds for specific alternative instructional programs, specifying transitional bilingual education (TBE) and developmental bilingual education (DBE) to be the two suggested instructional methods for ELLs. Cubillos (1988) defines both the programs as the following:

> **Transitional bilingual education programs** are designed for LEP students in elementary or secondary schools. These programs offer structured English instruction combined with, when necessary, instruction in the student's native language. The student's cultural heritage and that of other children in American society are included in the curriculum. These programs must provide instruction which allows students to meet grade promotion and graduation standards. To the extent possible, students are to be placed in classes with children of approximately the same age and level of educational attainment.
> **Developmental bilingual education programs** are full-time programs designed to provide structured English instruction and instruction in a second language. These programs must help students achieve competence in English or a second language while mastering subject matter skills that allow them to meet grade promotion and graduation standards. Where possible, classes shall include approximately equal numbers of students whose native language is English and students whose native language is the second language of instruction or study. (p. 1)

The saga of bilingual education continued through the development of this policy. Secretary Bennett "stressed that learning English is the key to equal opportunity and is the unifying bond for the diverse population of the United States." He advocated removing restrictions on the amount of bilingual education funds that could be devoted to the English-only School Assisted Instructional Program. In doing so, he attempted to remove funds specifically reserved for programs using students' native language. Although research evidence was presented to make a case against this change, Congress went along with the administration's recommendation and passed the bill (Lyons, 1995) against the use of first-language instruction.

During the Clinton administration, the direction of the bilingual education policy began to change. On October 20, 1994, President Clinton signed Title VII of the Elementary/Secondary Education Act (ESEA), which reauthorized the Bilingual Education Act as part of the Improving American Schools Act. This law contained significant changes and provisions to improve educational services for linguistically and culturally diverse students. For the first time, discretionary funding was provided for bilingual education through grants for capacity building in instruction, demonstration, research evaluation and dissemination, and program development and enhancement projects. The most important change in the new law was its recognition of the importance of bilingualism as a program outcome. It gave priority to program applications that provided for the development of bilingual proficiency in both English and another language. However, the 104th Congress considered legislation to "repeal the law, to eliminate its funding, and under a sweeping 'English only' proposal to outlaw most federal government operations in other languages . . . appropriations were reduced to 38% between 1994–96 . . ." (Crawford, 1997, p. 4). Then, in 1998, Congress passed the Riggs Bill, restricting the instruction of second language in many ways, and then passed the Educational Excellence for All Children Act of 1999. This law not only emphasized learning English for ELLs but also the need for reaching high academic standards like other regular students.

Finally, after President George W. Bush signed NCLB into a law on January 8, 2002, "it simplified federal support for ELL by combining categorical bilingual and immigrant education . . . into a State formula program . . . that will facilitate the comprehensive program that benefit all limited English proficient student by helping them learn English and meet the same high academic standards as other students" (Executive Summary, 2001, p. 2). This national effort to educate all children to high levels of academic achievement came with No Child Left Behind (NCLB) law requiring ELLs also to achieve the academic standards required for all.

> . . . children who are limited English proficient, including immigrant children and youth, attain English proficiency, develop high levels of academic attainment in English, and meet the same challenging State academic content and student academic achievement standards as all children are expected to meet. (NCLB, Title III, Part A, Sec. 3102. Purposes [1])
>
> All students will reach high standards, at a minimum attaining proficiency or better in reading and mathematics by 2013–2014. (California's version of NCLB states, all students will attain "proficiency" in reading and mathematics by 2014, including students with disabilities and English learners. All limited English proficient students will become proficient in English. (*Federal Register*, 2002)

NCLB has shifted the focus to accountability rather than effective instruction. It now emphasizes academic achievement and adequate yearly progress rather than achieving English language proficiency. It also enforces the "quick fix" of narrowing the gap between the majority and minority students rather than quality instruction that involves gradual development to assure academic success for all learners. In other words, this federal mandate implies that English as a second language be learned mainly through English instruction, which places greater demand on all teachers because the mainstream classroom has become the common learning place for all students including ELLs and students with special needs. Table 1.1 shows how the policy shaped the instructional program development and reveals an up-and-down trend between the use of first language plus English and the use of English only.

It can be summarized from this brief review of the federal bilingual policy for second-language instruction that for the past 35 years, the instruction of second-language learners has been dominated by the federal mandate that did not give priority to the pedagogy of second-language learning supported by research. Therefore, several types of instructional programs have been implemented in the schools to teach ELLs. Table 1.2 gives an overview of the various instructional program models for ELLs that have been tried in schools. It is clear here that the issue of second-language instruction has been shaped by educational policy that did not consider the research about second-language learning, which implies first-language proficiency as a prerequisite to efficient second-language learning (Crawford, 1995).

The cited list of instructional program models show clearly that the current policy context supports the latter three models of instruction in English for the content as well as learning the language arts skills at the elementary and secondary levels, implying English acquisition as the language goal for the schools. Although efforts were taken on and off by school districts to use bilingual instructional process for ELLs, the educational policy has worked very much against that. In the state of California, Proposition 227 barred bilingual education and pushed ELLs into structured English immersion classrooms, while in Arizona "English only" restrictions

TABLE 1.1 Instructional Implications in Bilingual Policy Development

Phases	Federal Bilingual Policy Stance on Instruction
Phase I (1968–1978)	• Began with vague and uncertain ideas of instruction but mainly as a funding source. • ESL and bilingual programs began to develop in schools. • Did not provide support for two-way bilingual programs. • Transitional bilingual program was supported.
Phase II (1978–1988)	• Importance of teaching English skills became the policy goal and quality of service became a policy priority. • After *Lau vs. Nicholas* the policy became more regulatory. More regulations for program development were tied to the funding. • Required structured English instruction in the program. At the same time encouraged transitional bilingual program—25% of the funding was set aside for special alternative instructional programs.
Phase II (1988–2002)	• A new policy direction occurred. ELLs were given access to the challenging curriculum and same educational standards as regular students. • Brought more rigorous academic requirements for ELL's academic achievement when it merged with NCLB as Title III. English proficiency has become a major goal, making accountability rather than pedagogy the focus. • Schools and teachers are held more accountable for showing academic achievement. • ELLs were to be tested like all learners to show academic achievement and improvement.

continue to burden the school and legislators refused to approve a budget that was equitable for ELLs (Crawford, 2006). Within this type of political milieu that is intensified by the NCLB requirements, schools are taking the responsibility of educating ELLs in the mainstream classroom. We have to raise our voice in support of the mainstream teachers who need the resources to build their capacity to teach all their students effectively.

According to a report resulting from the Civil Rights Project at Harvard University in February, 2005, the NCLB law has certainly brought many challenges for ELLs and the schools they attend because the law fails to acknowledge the research evidence that supports first-language proficiency as an important element in achieving second-language proficiency. In addition, the varied cultural background characteristics and the language proficiency of students do not match the assessment characteristics of the standardized tests, which were not normed for them. Besides, because of the resource inequities that exist between schools, those that serve a great number of ELLs do not have adequate instructional materials or efficiently trained teachers to serve them. In spite of these challenges, NCLB has a sweeping influence on schools, with many unintended consequences. One of them is the synergetic efforts to

TABLE 1.2   English as Second Language Instructional Models

Program Name	Language of Content Instruction	Language of Language Arts Instruction	Linguistic Goal
Two-way bilingual education or dual-language immersion	Both English and native language	English and the native language	Bilingualism
Late-exit or developmental bilingual education	All students speak the same native language. Mostly native language is used. Instruction through English increases as students gain proficiency.	English and native language	Bilingualism
Early-exit or transitional bilingual education	All students speak the same native language.	Both languages are used first, then a quick progression to all instruction in English.	English acquisition; rapid transfer into English-only classroom. (Supported by NCLB)
Sheltered English SDAIE Structured English immersion content-based ESL	English adapted to the students' proficiency level, and supplemented by gestures and visual aids.	English	English acquisition (Supported by NCLB)
Pull-out ESL	English adapted to the students' proficiency.	English	English acquisition (Supported by NCLB)

Source: Taken and modified from NCELA write-up on Introduction to Language Instructional Programs, http://www.ncela.gwu.edu/about/lieps/4_desc.html.

submerge ELLs into the English dominance of the mainstream classrooms and work on meeting the adequate yearly progress (AYP) and other accountability measures of NCLB.

"CAUGHT IN THE COCOON" PHENOMENON

The described historical account of ELLs in the mainstream class can be metaphorically described as the instruction of ELLs being a "caught in the cocoon" phenomenon. If a diagram of the life stages of a monarch butterfly is flashed before your eyes, you would first see the monarch growing from a tiny egg into a larva crawling on a leaf. Then, it develops a cocoon or chrysalis and cages itself to experience a transformative growth; its bright green color changes to dark blue and suddenly, a few days later, it breaks through the walls of the cocoon as a full-fledged monarch butterfly. As its wings dry, it flies to the nearest food spot. From then on, it experiences a freedom that is hard to imagine and flies away to live its full life.

This system of metamorphosis in a butterfly's life illustrates the crucial principle of change and progress from one stage to another, and in this path of progression a profound alteration occurs at one level that leads to full maturity. At the pupa stage the larva transforms itself into a butterfly, determining its destiny in the cocoon. If we look at the educational program development of ELLs, it is obvious that this development has been paralyzed by unresolved issues related to student placement in the available instructional programs, methods of instruction, and ways of monitoring their progress. Thus, the educational process for ELLs is caught in the "cocoon" of policy regulations and mandates that are not supported by research on second-language learning. Therefore, the instructional development for ELLs has not reached a full maturity. The progress is very slow, and in many ways it seems like the butterfly is unable to get out of the cocoon. The following diagram visually captures this dilemma:

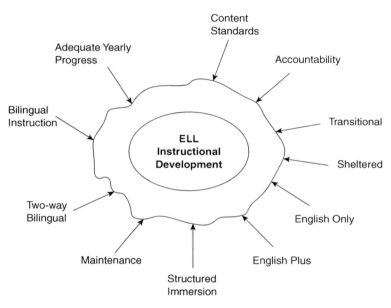

ELL Instruction caught in the middle.

It has become clear that since the enactment of the Bilingual Education Law in 1968 to the passing of NCLB in 2002 as a Title III program, debate has been continuous about the instruction of second language, with controversy over whether to teach English through first-language literacy and bilingual instruction or through English immersion to expedite English language proficiency. This debate has caused continuous tension between the ideas of assimilation and maintenance. Those who believe in the assimilation philosophy think that immigrants who speak languages other than English must learn English as quickly as possible. The maintenance philosophy, on the other hand, opposes the systemic and definite loss of the native language and culture in language minority children because this loss slows down the second-language learning process and violates the rights of ethnic groups to their identity as defined and expressed in their language and culture (Trueba, 1986). It proposes that the second language is best learned through the use of first language and culture, but the issue of how second-language development occurs proficiently did not become the instrumental factor of the policy.

Although the Bilingual Education Law was authorized six times before it merged with the NCLB, the theory and practice for second-language-instruction effectiveness have been questioned and efforts are continuously taken to discredit its necessity. This checkered history has contributed to the current ambiguous status of this field. Thus, a lack of consensus about the philosophy, goals, and expectations for instructional programs continues to haunt this field.

The current reforms have also called for increased accountability, requiring all students to have access to general education curriculum by including the English learners and special needs students in the statewide and district-level testing programs. To make it worse, in California, English-only tests are given to ELLs who still do not have English proficiency for academic success. Similarly, many states are establishing annual achievement objectives for all schools to measure the progress of all students and to hold schools accountable and increase graduation rates. Thus, the standards reform, NCLB, Proposition 227 in California, and other inclusion movements have raised the achievement bar sharply by mandating the responsibility of teaching ELLs and SNSs with all other students in the regular classroom. However, the dilemma of how best to deliver instruction that will contribute to English language development of ELLs remains unresolved. Consequently, it has become totally the responsibility of mainstream teachers to teach academic English and content knowledge to ELLs in their classrooms.

HISTORICAL DEVELOPMENT OF SPECIAL NEEDS LEARNER INSTRUCTION

The history of special education in the United States has its roots in the colonial period and has a different history than that of second-language instruction. The introduction of education to people with disabilities occurred during the early colonial times when rapid changes in education were taking place along with many social reforms. There was a gradual development of consciousness for social responsibility for the care of the disabled in the society. Institutions for teaching the deaf and blind populations popped up in various places. In 1850, the Massachusetts School for Idiotic and Feeble-Minded Children was established by the state legislature, and soon after, New York State funded its first school for children with mental retardation (Winzer, 2002). Soon special institutions were established for children with handicapping conditions, and these were administered as part of the social welfare division. For many decades that followed, institutionalizing the special needs population became the only way of treating them. Institutions for the deaf, blind, and mentally retarded flourished as colonies expanded, and profound social change began to occur as more immigrants poured into the communities.

Then, as educational progress occurred in American schools and the professionalization of teaching developed, concern for the education of the handicapped also grew stronger. Teacher training institutions began to add courses for preparing teachers for students with disabilities, and segregated classes for such individuals appeared. However, lack of trained teachers became apparent and many special classes failed in their efforts at remediation of children who did not conform to a "school's behavioral standards" (Rhodes & Sagor, 1975).

In the early 1900s, a reconceptualization of human disabilities occurred and handicapping conditions were no longer considered as illnesses but more as disabilities. There was also a growing awareness about school attendance and compulsory schooling for all children, including the deaf and blind. Many states implemented compulsory attendance laws for all students that included the deaf and blind children, passed legislation authorizing special education, and set forth legal requirements for teacher certification. Schools were required to teach all children who enrolled, which meant a great number of children with varied abilities and diverse learning difficulties entered regular schools. Gradually, special classes became part of the educational setting. No longer could schools direct individuals with disabilities to institutions because there was a growing agreement about disabled students needing "community based facilities rather than institutional isolation" (Wallin, 1924, p. 122).

In addition, progressive educational reform spurred the idea of curriculum differentiation in schools and brought to the forefront concern for educating special needs learners. Curriculum and instruction included individual attention and guidance to emphasize remedial, corrective, or differential instruction to meet the varying needs of students through special classes. Segregation in special classes for disabled children was considered vital for the undisturbed learning of mainstream children (Prattt, 1920). Moreover, IQ tests were used as the measure for placement in special segregated classes. This was the beginning of diagnosis and classification of special education students. Growth of special classes continued through the 1930s as categories of special needs children also increased. The idea of segregating special needs students in special classes in the same schools where regular students attended became a well-established practice. In the meantime, many states authorized special education and set forth legal requirements for teacher certification to allow teacher training institutions to offer coursework on teaching the exceptional child. Special curricula designed to meet the needs of children in a growing number of different categories of exceptionality were also developed, and special education became an area of specialization in professional education (Winzer, 2002).

In the 1950s, the perception of educating special needs students began to change. Public concerns were raised and consciousness was directed toward providing individuals with mental retardation with the same opportunities available to ordinary citizens. "Several landmark legal decisions designed to safeguard the basic human rights of mentally retarded individuals established as their constitutional rights such principles as due process, equal protection under the law . . ." (Rosen, Clark, & Kivitz, 1976). As enrollments in special education program swelled, parent advocacy groups developed into a powerful legislative lobby.

In the 1960s during the Kennedy era, the federal government moved toward providing financial assistance for research on disabilities that resulted in the formation of the Bureau of Education for the Handicapped. President Kennedy also signed P.L. 88–164 in October 1963, which broadened the special education population to include not only the mentally retarded but also those who had any type of disability. Other public laws were passed to authorize and institutionalize special education in our schools. Federal financial assistance also was assured, but special education learners still were mainly taught in specially segregated settings—and that was believed to be the best educational arrangement for them.

However, P.L. 94–142 of 1974 had a new philosophy and focus. "Under this legislation exceptional children were, for the first time, accorded the right to a free and appropriate education in the least restrictive environment. Their parents or guardians were given the right of due process and confidentiality, and school boards were mandated to provide a range of educational services, an individual educational plan for every exceptional student, and culturally fair testing" (Winzer, 2002, p. 382).

This brought about a major change in the instruction of special education learners in our schools. No longer could schools send special needs learners to self-contained classrooms or segregated special programs. They were required to organize a school team made up of the school psychologist, counselor, social worker, teachers, and administrator to plan individual educational plans (IEPs) for learning in the least restrictive environment. This law brought the major push for integrating special needs learners into the mainstream classrooms. Since then schools have been mandated not to segregate the special needs learners into self-contained classrooms but rather to include them in the inclusive environment of the mainstream classroom as much as possible.

This legal mandate was strengthened further by the Education for All Handicapped Children Act in 1976–1977 and the Individuals with Disabilities Education Act (IDEA) in 1989–1990, which both support the idea that students with disabilities should be educated in regular classrooms for the maximum amount of time possible. This law emphasized the school working to meet all the needs of the special students (Taylor & Harrington, 2003). For the past 20 or more years, special education students have been treated with equity in education through the least restrictive environment (LRE). This social movement began by bringing adults and children with disabilities from state institutions to the public school and community programs. Now it has influenced the inclusion of special needs students in the mainstream classroom. In addition to that, NCLB has become the catalyst for holding the teachers and students accountable for their academic performance. These have become the major demands of NCLB, thus making the instruction of special needs learners a mainstream classroom concern. "Beginning with the IDEA amendments in 1997 through the current amendments, coupled with NCLB, we are moving back to the traditional standard of sameness" (Weintraub, 2005, p. 97).

It is important here to specify that students with serious handicaps are not usually mainstreamed. Special needs students in general are described according to their disability and classified into various categories. For example, students with disabilities are grouped on the basis of their major handicap and they are classified as follows: "1. Mentally handicapped, 2. learning disabled, 3. emotionally unstable, 4. traumatic brain injury and 5. socially maladjusted health impairments (those with special or language defects), 6. blind and hard of seeing, 7. deaf and hard of hearing, 8. orthopedic impairments, 9. those with special health impairments and multiple handicapped" (Taylor & Harrington, 2003, p. 43). "Disabled students with serious types of exceptionalities such as emotional disturbance, visual impairments, hearing impairments, mental retardation, and deaf-blindness have been educated in inclusive settings to some degree; however, most of them are educated in separate school settings" (Taylor & Harrington, 2003, p. 150). Those who are mainstreamed do not have serious exceptionalities. They come from the high-incident learning disabled, emotionally impaired, attention deficit disorder, and other mildly impaired conditions. Besides, in today's classrooms, children who are not able to pay attention to teaching and stay on the learning tasks until completion are also categorized as special needs learners. "Some of these children are diagnosed with attention-deficit hyperactivity disorder (ADHD). It is estimated that approximately three to five percent of the United States school age population is affected by attention-deficit hyperactivity disorder" (Rupley & Nichols, 1998, p. 248).

However, efforts to provide the least restrictive learning environments to all these types of learners is a major thrust of the current educational policy. In a speech by Robert H. Pasternack (2002), assistant secretary for Special Education and Rehabilitative Services, that message was very obvious. He stated the following:

> Today, the overwhelming majority of children with disabilities—about 96 percent—learn in regular schools with other children rather than in State institutions or separate facilities. Three-quarters of students with disabilities now spend at least 40 percent of their day in a regular classroom with their non-disabled peers, instead of in separate rooms. Half of the students with disabilities spend 80 percent or more of their day in regular classrooms. Additionally, more students with disabilities than ever before are participating in the same State, district-wide, and national standardized testing programs as other students.

Moreover, it is stated that an essential goal of special education is for students to "demonstrate competency in challenging subject matter and learn to use their minds well, so that they may be prepared for responsible citizenship, further learning, and productive employment" (Taylor & Harrington, 2003, p. 58). It is intended that this goal will be achieved in the mainstream classroom by the mainstream teacher. Thus, it is very clear that the movement to "push" the special needs learners into the regular classrooms has gained momentum and schools are making all-out efforts to follow this mandate.

CHAPTER SUMMARY

This brief historical review of policies and programs related to the schooling of ELLs and SNSs clearly establishes the fact that through educational reform efforts the mainstream classroom has become the final learning ground for these students, and their academic success has become a matter of teacher accountability. The responsibility of teaching the academic content standards and leading all students to academic achievement at grade level has become a major responsibility of the regular teacher in the mainstream classroom. This "tall order" calls for a change in the instructional role of the mainstream teachers because the traditional type of mainstream teaching is no longer viable. Classroom teachers are in essence being asked to develop a positive pedagogical approach to their teaching and create a learning culture that accommodates the learning differences of all their learners. That requires teachers to embark on a learning journey. As independent "artisans" and professionals, they must build up their knowledge, skills, abilities, dispositions, and habits of mind and engage in continuous learning and professional development to hone and adapt their teaching to meet student learning demands (Sykes, 1999).

REFERENCES

Abedi, J. (2004). The No Child Left Behind Act and English language learners: Assessment and accountability issues. *Educational Researcher, 33*(1), 4–14.

Alexander, K., & Alexander, M. (1992). *American public law.* New York: West Publishing Company.

Batt, L., Kim, J., & Sunderman, G. (2005). Limited English students: Increased accountability under NCLB. Policy brief. Civil Rights Project at Harvard University.

Casanova, U. (1995). Bilingual education: Politics or pedagogy? In O. Garcia & C. Baker (Eds.), *Policy and practice in bilingual education*. Philadelphia: Multilingual Matters.

Crawford, J. (1995) *Bilingual education: History, politics, theory and practice*. Los Angeles, CA: Bilingual Educational Services.

Crawford, J. (1997). *Best evidence: Research foundations of the Bilingual Education Act*. Washington, DC: National Clearinghouse for Bilingual Education.

Crawford, J (2006). NABE 2006 in political context. *Language Learnerm, 1*(4), 2.

Cummins, J. (1986). Empowering minority students: A framework for intervention. *Harvard Education Review, 15*, 18–36.

Cummins, J. (1996). *Negotiating identities: Education for empowerment in a diverse society*. Los Angeles: California Association for Bilingual Education.

Darling-Hammond, L. (2004). From "Separate but Equal" to "No Child Left Behind": The collision of new standards and old inequalities. In D. Meier and G. Wood (Eds.), *Many children left behind*. Boston, MA: Beacon Press.

Democrat-Chronicle. (1981, March 8). Rochester, p. 2A.

Fuchs, D., & Fuchs, L. (1994) Inclusive schools movement and the radicalization of special education reform. *The Council for Exceptional Children. 60*(4), 294–309.

Gottlieb, M. *Evidence-based teaching strategies for achieving academic English and content . . . The theory behind the research*. Illinois Resource Center & WIDA Consortium.

Introduction to language educational programs. Available online at http://www.ncela.gwu.edu/about/lieps.

Kirk, S., & Gallaher, J. (1983). *Educating exceptional children*. Dallas, TX: Houghton Mifflin Company.

Leibowitz, A. (1980). *The Bilingual Education Act: A legislative analysis*. Rosslyn, VA: National Clearinghouse for Bilingual Education.

Lyons, J. (l995). The past and future directions of federal bilingual-educational policy. In O. Garcia & C. Baker (Eds.), *Policy and practice in bilingual education*. Philadelphia: Multilingual Matters LTD.

Merrit, S. Clearing the hurdles of inclusion. *Educational Leadership, 59*(3), 67–70.

Ovando, J., & Collier, V. (l985). *Bilingual and ESL classrooms: Teaching in multicultural contexts*. New York: McGraw-Hill Book Company.

Poplin, M., & Weeres, J. (1992). Voices from the inside: A report of schooling from classroom.

Rhodes, W. C., & Sagor, M. (1975). Community perspectives. In N. Hobbs (Ed.), *Issues in the classification of children* (Vol. 1). San Francisco: Jossey Bass.

Rosen, M., Clark, G., & Kivitz, M. (l976). *The history of mental retardation*. Baltiomore: University Park Press.

Sacco, J. (2002). Special-needs solutions. *Instructor, 114*(4), 16.

Taylor, G., & Harrington, F. (2003). *Educating the disabled*. Lanham, MD: Scarecrow Education.

Trueba, H. (1986). Raising silent voices: *Educating the linguistic minorities for the 21st century*.

Valenzuela, A. (1999). *Subtractive schooling: U.S. Mexican youth and the politics of caring*. Albany: State University of New York Press.

Wallin, J. (1924). *The education of handicapped children*. Boston, MA: Houghton Mifflin.

Weintraub, F. (2005). The evolution of LD policy and future challenges. *Learning Disability Quarterly, 28*(2), 97–99.

Winzer, M. (2002). *The history of special education*. Washington, DC: Gallaudet University Press.

CHAPTER 2

Making Instructional Adaptation as an Equity Solution: What, Why, and How?

We believe that there are no excuses now for not attempting to discover ways to facilitate learning and connect classroom experiences more effectively with our students, especially ELLs and SNSs (Solomon, Lalas, & Franklin, 2006). Although the realistic impact of the existing social, economic, language, and learning differences between mainstream students and the English language and special needs learners contributes to the ever-widening gap in academic achievement (Kozol, 2005; Popham, 2004), we believe that through academic content adaptation we can provide equity solutions to meet the instructional needs of all students and narrow that achievement gap (Barone, 2006; Haycock, Jerald, & Huang, 2001; Portes, 2005; Singham, 2003). This is an ambitious task given the fact that "there are only a few isolated ethnographies and other studies that demonstrate practical ways for schools and educators to work productively with students from diverse economic, ethnic, cultural, and linguistic backgrounds" (Edwards & Schmidt, 2006).

In her foreword for the book entitled *Making Race Visible: Literacy Research for Cultural Understanding*, Ladson-Billings (2003) asserted that we have done enough reporting and interpreting of injustice and inequity. We believe that making an academic content adaptation is one way of taking our obligation into action. In our book's particular framework—making adaptation as an equity solution—we go beyond "recipes," "quick-fixes," or "add-ons" in providing the English language and special needs learners access to academic content.

In this chapter, we present making adaptation as an intentional teaching event grounded in theory and best practice in the areas of teacher efficacy (Ashton, 1984) and "ethic of caring" (Collier, 2005; Noddings, 1992), teacher learning (Darling-Hammond & McLaughlin, 1999;

Elmore & Burney, 1999), teaching for social justice (Adams, Bell, & Griffin, 1997; Brown, 2004; Cochran-Smith, 2004; Marshall & Oliva, 2006; Michelli & Keiser, 2005; Rodgers, 2006), working with diverse learners (Moll & Gonzalez, 2001; Nieto, 2000, 2003; Salazar-Stanton, 2001; Trueba, 1999; Valenzuela, 1999), and language, literacy, and academic language development (Lee & Lalas, 2003). Our adaptation framework uses the sociocognitive model of reading that reflects the dynamic interaction among the learner, the teacher, and the classroom context (Ruddell & Unrau, 2004). It also places reliance on the role of teacher reflection in making instructional decisions (Schon, 1987; Tremmel, 1993).

WHAT IS ACADEMIC CONTENT ADAPTATION?

Academic content adaptation is a process of knowing and making relevant and appropriate plans for students who have special needs or abilities, including the English language and special needs learners, to make subject matter comprehensible, engage and support students in learning, and create effective environments for learning. Making adaptation implies the creation of a relevant and appropriate yet challenging learning experience where all students feel safe, comfortable, trusted, confident, and respected for who they are, what identity they take on, what level of academic proficiency they bring, and the cultural beliefs and ideals they uphold. The teacher in this process believes in his or her ability to make a difference in student success by taking personal responsibility for student learning and developing improved strategies to meet his or her students' needs (Ashton, 1984).

In making adaptation, the teacher is expected to be knowledgeable of subject-matter content, aware of the social, economic, linguistic, and cultural factors that affect learning, and able to recognize the need for students to acquire a deeper understanding of the instructional material in order to make it relevant to their lives. Only with this background can a teacher attempt to make any effective adjustment or modification to the general education program that could enable students with special learning circumstances to participate in and benefit from content-standard-based learning activities and experiences. In addition, an effective instructional adaptation encourages and motivates students to excel academically by providing them with equitable opportunities to gain access to curriculum at their own pace.

Indeed, making instructional adaptation is a clear indicator of a teacher's disposition to care about student learning. From the perspective of "ethic of caring" (Noddings, 1992), the caring role of a teacher is similar to that of "mothering" and includes the protection, nurturing, and shaping of the growth of the child. Collier (2005) emphasizes the importance of the "ethic of caring" as a motivating and influential force for teacher efficacy—a teacher's belief in his or her ability to make a difference in student learning—as well as the purposeful and intentional instructional decisions teachers make in their classrooms. A caring teacher is committed to his or her students, constantly improves his or her pedagogical skills and content knowledge to meet the needs of the students, establishes trusts with his or her students, and models how to care for the well-being of others.

Similarly, Darling-Hammond and Baratz-Snowden (2005, p. 5) explain that a good teacher in every classroom must acquire the following three general areas of knowledge:

- knowledge of learners and how they learn and develop within social contexts
- understanding of the subject matter and skills to be taught in light of the social purposes of education
- understanding of teaching in light of the content and learners to be taught, as informed by assessment and supported by a productive environment

These three essential areas of knowledge provide teachers with a framework for understanding teaching and learning, including the content, context, and process of making instructional adaptation to make learning accessible to English language learners and students with special needs.

MAKING ADAPTATION IS AN INTERACTIVE PROCESS

There are essential elements that influence the development of a teacher's set of knowledge, abilities, skills, and dispositions in working with all students, including English language and special needs learners. These elements include a positive classroom context, the teacher's set of personal prior experiences and pedagogical skills, and the teacher's knowledge of his or her student backgrounds. As teachers consciously use their skills, knowledge of their students, and understanding of the classroom context, they become effective in providing equity solutions for all students, especially the English language learners and special needs students. Consequently, they create classroom conditions that depict a just, equitable, and culturally responsive learning environment. The equity solution that teachers provide their ELLs and SNSs will in turn educate them within a "democratic" teaching context so that, as future citizens, they become full participants in political, civic, and economic life.

Making adaptation as an interactive process becomes an important and conscious decision-making mechanism that helps the development of a teacher to become intentional, passionate, and purposeful in making academic matters accessible and the pupils engaged in what they do to achieve their best. The teacher's willingness to learn new ways of teaching and become receptive to theory-based and research-based information are key ingredients in providing equity opportunities for English language and special needs students in a positive learning environment where both the pupils and their teacher are making content comprehensible through their active interaction and adaptation. It is imperative to understand that a vital element in making academic content adaptation is the interactive connection between a teacher's set of knowledge, skills, and abilities and the students' prior knowledge and academic, literacy, and language skills, as well as their overall personal abilities. This interaction happens in the classroom context that includes all the media, materials, tasks, assignments, and sources of information, decision, or authority.

We learned from Ruddell and Unrau's (2004) sociocognitive cognitive model of reading that the interaction among its three major components involves the reader, text and classroom context, and the teacher. Applied to working with the English language and special needs learners, the dynamic interplay between what experiences and academic capabilities these learners bring to the classroom and what teacher learning backgrounds a teacher has plays significant roles in facilitating academic access and the construction of meaningful and purposeful knowledge.

This viable current perspective in literacy development shows that the **dynamic interaction of the teacher, the learner, and the classroom context** is the driving force for the motivation to acquire academic content knowledge and engagement in collaborative inquiry (Ruddell & Unrau, 2004). The building of teacher-learner relationships—the positive forging and elaboration of interpersonal dynamics related to issues of authority, role, power, status, and the interrogation and determination of views about what and whose knowledge is of most value—are embedded in this dynamic interaction. Similarly, teacher reflection, a cognitive process that includes problem solving, inferencing, activation of prior knowledge and beliefs, and decision making, also plays a very important role in making the necessary instructional decision that leads to adaptation for academic content comprehension and acquisition. It is the process that allows both the teacher and the learner to deliberately connect ideas based on their beliefs and knowledge of the classroom context, evaluate past interaction or practice, assess weaknesses and strengths, and create an atmosphere of openness for instructional adaptation.

WHY IS MAKING ADAPTATION AN EQUITY SOLUTION?

According to England (2005), "equity and respect are interrelated . . . and the foundations for justice and for learning." She describes with concrete examples the inequities plaguing our school system that may disproportionately affect the education of the English language and special education students: inequity within diversity, inequity within assessment, inequity within standards, and inequity in curriculum. She further asserts that "when a society treats the mass of people in this way, singling out only a few for recognition, it creates a scarcity of respect, as though there were not enough of this precious substance to go around. Like many famines, this scarcity is man-made" (England, 2005, p. xiv).

We believe that it is incumbent upon teachers to create classroom conditions that convey respect for all students. Making instructional adaptation as a conscious approach conveys respect to what learners bring in the instructional contexts and provides them with productive opportunities to engage actively with the curriculum, instructional delivery, classroom assessment, and overall academic content. Making adaptation as an equity solution starts with the recognition that there are specific cultural characteristics that all students, including the English language and special needs learners, bring to the learning process. For example, even though determined initially to be influential in the school performance of English language learners, certain factors such as "funds of knowledge," politics of caring, and social networking should have strong impacts on building resiliency, character, and self-identity for academic success for both English learners and special needs students. There should always be a consistent and systematic attention to incorporate the students' background knowledge in curriculum and instructional delivery to strengthen their self-identity.

The term "funds of knowledge" refers to students' lived experiences in their homes, schools, and communities. The variety of multiple identities students have, their social backgrounds, and their overall experiences are dynamic sources of "funds of knowledge" (Moll, Amanti, Neff, & Gonzalez, 1992; Moll & Gonzalez, 2001). Research has shown that the English language learners have a variety of community and household experiences that shape the strengths they bring into classrooms. One research study identified *confianza* (mutual trust) as a glue that held together the social relationships and "culture of caring" among administrators, teachers, and students (Moll & Arnot-Hopffer, 2005). We can only infer here at this point that it may also be true with the special needs students. The notion of funds of knowledge implies that there are always networks of friends, relatives, and other community contacts that facilitate different types of economic assistance, labor cooperation and referral, and societal advancement and participation. It is essential that teachers acknowledge these "funds of knowledge" and teach students how to use these resources to facilitate their acquisition of skills and knowledge and nurture their learning and intellectual advancement.

It is well established in research related to English language learners that the students' interconnections—including background knowledge, schools, families, neighborhoods, communities, and overall lived experiences that they have acquired—provide the solid foundation for their social and intellectual development. Teachers should learn how to build from the "funds of knowledge" students already have by openly acknowledging diversity in language, culture, gender, ethnicity, sexual orientation, and class backgrounds as valuable points of reference. For students with special needs, teachers should attempt to draw the implications of "funds of knowledge" as considerations for matching instruction with students' backgrounds and lived experiences.

Another factor that has positive influence in the educational performance of diverse students is the politics of caring and connectedness they experience with their teachers, counselors, and friends. Valenzuela (1999) describes "politics of caring" as the potential reciprocal relations of respect and support between students and educators. She explains that diverse students and teachers need to develop positive feelings of trust and nurture meaningful relationships in order to enhance their learning and academic success. She asserts that diverse students have to be *cared for,* respected, and valued by their peers, teachers, and administrators before they can *care about* school. Research has shown that students who have strong caring connections with friends and school personnel including their teachers and counselors are "more likely to resist the pull of gangs that offer an alternative form of connection for alienated students" (Goldstein & Soriano, 1994; Oscher & Fleischman, 2005, p. 84).

Social networking is another factor that has powerful impact in the schooling of minority and other diverse students. Stanton-Salazar (2001) explains the need for diverse students to create social connections with "institutional agents" such as teachers, counselors, and mentors who can help them navigate through the educational system for new and better educational opportunities. While student *ganas* (motivation) and potentials are important, the assistance provided by these institutional agents can serve to guide their overall progress in the highly competitive and complex urban learning environments. Stanton-Salazar (2001) also recognizes the significant role of parents and encourages language minority students to develop forms of identity that can serve to strengthen their social values, bridge cultures, and allow them to excel academically.

The diverse students' backgrounds related to factors such as their funds of knowledge, connectedness, and social networking contribute to the development of student resiliency. As teachers make instructional adaptations in teaching the diverse students, it is paramount for them to consciously think about the process, content, and context of building that resiliency. Nieto (1999) cites studies that linked supportive networks of teachers and friends to the academic success of

Hispanic students. Personal relationships that develop between teachers and minority students serve as "protective networks" that strengthen and motivate students to achieve. Trueba (1999) explains the notion of cultural resiliency as a process by which immigrant children and their families learn to rely upon their culture, family, friends, and ethnic community as sources of support and cultural shields from discriminatory treatments.

Teachers should recognize the notion of resiliency so that they may be guided on how to complement and build the students' positive personal traits, self-esteem, and dispositions as they plan, implement, and assess academic content instruction for the English language and special needs students. Generally, students who maintain a strong self-identity with their social and cultural community are able to do well in school in spite of social inequities.

MAKING ADAPTATION IS TEACHING FOR EDUCATIONAL JUSTICE

As teachers make instructional adaptation to provide English language and special needs learners access to academic curriculum and instruction, they are serving as advocates for equity, positive behavior, caring connections, resiliency, funds of knowledge, and effective learning for diverse students. Subsequently, through careful attention to the needs of these diverse students and knowledge of how to engage them productively in a highly complex academic learning environment, English language learners and students with special needs become connected participants in the classroom culture and active users and consumers of the curriculum. Teachers have the ultimate opportunity and responsibility to involve diverse students in worthy and comprehensible activities that promote the recognition of the value of each individual in the classroom and create learning environments that are democratic, just, equitable, and caring. Making instructional adaptation is an opportunity for teaching for social justice, or in a narrower classroom context, a tool to teach for *educational justice*.

We believe that aside from knowledge of subject matter, knowledge of learners, and knowledge of teaching, teaching involves personal passion, vision, virtue, and commitment in making content accessible to all students by all means, including the English language and special needs learners. The notions of equity, diversity, and social justice should not be empty "add-ons" in a program curriculum. They must be put into action through explicit instructional strategies that are adaptable to the needs of all students in highly diverse classrooms.

Cochran-Smith (2004) explains the transformation in knowledge, skills, abilities, and disposition that teachers need personally to teach for social justice. The list of "social justice" instructional agenda includes culturally responsive teaching; comprehensible and accessible content; effective and purposeful questioning; use of different forms assessment to inform instruction; support for students; collaboration with parents, community members, and other professionals; knowledge of how to interpret data; maintenance of high academic standards; possession of teacher-researcher qualities; and strong advocacy for equity. She asserts that teaching from a social justice perspective is not a matter of simply transmitting knowledge and equating pupil learning to higher scores on high-stakes tests, but rather engaging pupils in "developing critical habits of mind, understanding and sorting out multiple perspectives, and learning to participate in and contribute to a democratic society by developing both the skill and the inclination for civic engagement" (Cochran-Smith, 2004, p. 159).

According to Noguera (2005), we neglect to consider the conditions under which students learn. While the mainstream students' experiences, academic abilities, language, culture, and economic status match the learning contexts of the school, many of our diverse students are not reaching their academic potential. He explains that simply listing schools by the percentage of students on free and reduced lunch provides us with knowledge about a school's potential academic rankings and the race and class makeup of the school. He asserts that "we do provide all children with access to school in this country—public education remains the only social entitlement in this country—but we get unequal education" (Noguera, 2005, p. 14).

WHAT DOES PROMOTING EDUCATIONAL JUSTICE IN THE CLASSROOM REALLY MEAN?

Making instructional adaptations promotes social justice in schools by providing ample opportunities to recognize and articulate the existing inequalities, respecting differences in race or ethnicity, cultural traditions and beliefs, social norms, intellectual flexibility, and personal perspectives and utilizing students' background knowledge into consideration in working with diverse students. Social justice can be cultivated in students by recognizing and honoring diversity, appreciating equity, advancing critical thinking and openness, and encouraging individual voice and unique expression (Brooks & Thompson, 2005).

Similarly, school counselors view an emphasis on social justice as an important skill in assuming an advocacy role as part of their work and their attention to social, political, and economic realities of students and families (Bemak & Chung, 2005). In the area of educational administration, Brown (2004) offers a practical, process-oriented model that is responsive to the challenges of preparing leaders committed to social justice and equity. She explains that being an administrator and leader for social justice requires grounding in learning theories, transformative pedagogy, and critical discourse and reflection—it aims to perceive contradictions and to take action against the oppressive elements of reality, and prepares to "work with and guide others in translating their perspectives, perceptions, and goals into agendas for social change" (p. 99).

Whatever view is used in explaining the term, a strong argument needs to be made for "the necessity of a social justice agenda in a democratic and increasingly diverse society" (Cochran-Smith, 2004, p. 168) and the emphasis on equity, ethical values, justice, care, and respect in educating students and educational leaders (Marshall & Oliva, 2006). Promoting social justice can also be framed as a lifelong undertaking that involves understanding oneself in relation to others; examining how privilege or inequality affects one's own opportunities as well as those of different people; exploring varied experiences and how those inform a person's unique worldview, perspectives, and opportunities; and evaluating how schools and classrooms can operate to value diverse human experiences and enable learning for all students (Darling-Hammond, French & Garcia-Lopez, 2002; Darling-Hammond & Baratz-Snowden, 2005).

Darling-Hammond and Baratz-Snowden (2005) imply that teachers for social justice need to understand their own identity, other people's background and their worldviews, and the sources of inequities and privileges. Commitment to these issues will assist school leaders in authentically facilitating the learning of students in their schools and making a difference in the lives of teachers and students.

Bell (1997) presents, in a more philosophical sense, that promoting social justice means providing all individuals and groups in a society with full and equal participation in meeting their needs. According to Bell, a just society is where the "distribution of resources is equitable and all members are physically and psychologically safe and secure" (p. 1). She explains that "social justice involves social actors who have a sense of their own agency as well as a sense of social responsibility toward and with others and the society as a whole" (p.1).

It is clear from Bell's conceptualization that educators who are committed to the practice of social justice need to understand that all individuals in the society must be responsible to each other and deserve to enjoy equity, security, safety, and involvement in their interactions and dealings with others and the society. Applied more specifically to teaching, Cochran-Smith (2000, 2004) frames promoting social justice in education as a conception of teaching and learning that includes the following instructional agenda: (1) learning to represent complex knowledge in accessible and culturally responsive ways, (2) learning to ask good questions, (3) using diversified forms of assessment to shape curriculum and instruction, (4) developing relationships with students that support and sustain learning, (5) working with—not against—parents and community members, (6) collaborating with other professionals, (7) interpreting multiple data sources in support of pupils' learning, (8) maintaining high academic standards for students of all abilities and backgrounds, (9) engaging in classroom inquiry in the service of pupil and teacher learning, and (10) joining with others in larger movements for educational and social equity.

We view social justice as a vehicle for educational justice in K–12 educational settings. Classroom teachers need to understand, value, and advocate for diversity and social justice because they are the foundations for providing *all* students with equitable educational learning environments (Brooks & Thompson, 2005). It is personal commitment, passion, and virtue for social justice that teachers need in order to create effective academic content adaptation for English language learners and students with special needs.

MAKING ADAPTATION FACILITATES LANGUAGE, LITERACY, AND ACADEMIC DEVELOPMENT

Second-language learners and students with special needs represent a large percentage of our students in K–12 schools. These groups of students face learning difficulty every day and are at risk because of certain factors related to their families' socioeconomic status, attendance in substandard schools, membership in special education classes, and negative self-concept. These factors in turn impact these students' performance in their subject-matter classes, literacy, language development, testing, and overall academic achievement. We argue in this chapter that making adaptation is a key solution to the challenges faced by students who have special language and learning needs. Teachers play significant roles in spearheading this classroom-based innovation because making academic content adaptation is directly in their hands. They are the ones who will orchestrate the dynamic interaction among the students, the classroom context, and themselves to achieve active engagement and academic productivity in school classrooms.

English language learners need effective instruction in situations where language is a barrier to their learning. Special needs students require differentiated instruction to enable them to benefit from learning activities and experiences based on the required curriculum content standards. Without a conscious effort on the part of the teacher to meet these needs, the English language and special needs learners will fall behind their peers in language, literacy, and academic development. For example, an English language learner entering first grade may be as much as 5,000 vocabulary words behind other students. About 80% of those special needs students diagnosed as having a learning disability have a serious problem in literacy and academic development (Gunning, 2005). Many strategies exist to close the achievement gap, especially the literacy gap. These research-based ideas and strategies include fostering vocabulary development and interest in words, teaching thinking skills with focus on comprehension, improving access to texts, building fluency, emphasizing caring and high expectations, instituting smaller class sizes, using paraeducators and parents, creating responsive classrooms, and engaging in data-driven professional development (Coelho, 2004; Gunning, 2006; Rhodes, Ochoa, & Ortiz, 2005; Young & Hadaway, 2006).

How do we make academic content adaptation to facilitate language, literacy, and academic development for English language and special needs learners? We start with a set of research-based and research-related concepts and "best practices." The concepts that grounded our making adaptation as an equity solution framework include the sociocognitive model of reading, teaching for social justice, funds of knowledge, culture of connectedness and caring, social networking, resiliency, working with English language and special needs learners, and diversity. From understanding the crucial elements embedded in these concepts as they relate to learning, language, literacy, and academic development, we created an academic content adaptation framework and set of procedures (Gordon, Lalas, & McDermott, 2006). We worked with a small group of teachers and pilot tested these adaptation procedures in their self-contained classrooms. We are reporting what we found in these experienced teachers' practice in comparison with preservice teachers, as discussed in the next chapter.

INSTRUCTIONAL ADAPTATION: HOW DO WE REALLY DO IT?

Essential in making instructional adaptation is the process of critical inquiry, with reflection as the key process. We believe that in order for teachers to upgrade their knowledge, teach with appropriate and relevant skills, abilities, and dispositions, and be able to think critically about students and their learning, **they have to learn to reflect.** Teacher reflection must include a critical understanding of the important roles played by their own experiential backgrounds, their students' identities and levels of academic and language proficiency, and the classroom contexts and tasks or assignments. Reflection helps teachers to look at instructional dilemmas carefully and equitably and think about how best they can manage teaching all learners, including ELLs and SNSs.

The notion of teacher reflection that we mean here is the kind that is practical and implies "thinking on your feet" (Schon, 1983, p. 42). The reflection process driving our adaptation framework consists of knowing the learners or students, knowing the subject-matter standards and goals, and knowing how to teach, assess, and manage diverse learners.

Evaluate Your ELL and Special Needs Students' Abilities to Engage in the Following:

Recognizing Individuality

*Does your student work comfortably by her- or himself?

*Do you think he or she has self-confidence in completing the work individually?

Knowing Who They Are in Relation to Others

*Does your student enjoy working with others?

*Do you think he or she can work productively with another student?

Working Together with Others in the Group as a Learning Community

*Does your student work well in groups?

*Do you think he or she can thrive in group situations?

Students as Problem Solvers, Critical Thinkers, and Risk Takers

*Does your student show eagerness in solving problems and thinking critically for solutions?

*Do you think he or she is a risk taker?

Independence in Applying and Demonstrating Knowledge

*Does your student demonstrate independence in applying the concepts learned in the various subject-matter areas?

*Do you think he or she shows success in applying and demonstrating knowledge?

Students as Reflective Participants in the Learning Process

*Does your student think about the consequences of his or her actions?

*Do you think he or she is able to identify the strengths and weaknesses of his or her performance?

Figure 2.1   Making adaptation: You have to know your students!

Knowledge about the students also includes specific information related to their linguistic and cultural backgrounds, academic language abilities and content knowledge related to subject matter, interests, and other relevant physical, social, and emotional development information.

It is important that preservice and inservice teachers identify the necessary formal and informal assessment tools that they can use to know who their students are and what knowledge, skills, and abilities they bring to the classroom.

MAKING ADAPTATION: CATEGORIES OF ADAPTATIONS

Teacher reflection is facilitated by knowing the types, forms, or categories of adaptations and common practical literacy strategies as well as technology resources available to them. Chapter 3 will show how preservice and inservice teachers use the different categories in their adaptations for English language and special needs learners. Chapter 4 will cover the adaptable literacy and technology support activities and resources. The current chapter shares the categories that we have learned from our classroom practice and other published work (New Jersey World Languages Curriculum Framework 1999).

Adaptations can be planned to take place before the presentation of the lesson, during the lesson, and after the completion of the lesson. It is therefore vital that instructional adaptations be viewed as a set of activities that helps facilitate access to subject-matter content before, during, and after a predetermined class lesson. Adaptations are alternative means for English language and special needs learners to acquire knowledge and exhibit their knowledge. The adaptation activities must compensate for the students' learning needs.

The New Jersey World Languages Curriculum Framework lists four categories of adaptations for pupils with disabilities: (1) instructional presentation, (2) classroom organization, (3) student response, and (4) student motivation. Instructional presentation involves teacher-initiated and teacher-directed interventions that prepare, prompt, promote and/or monitor student learning and engagement. Classroom organization includes modification in the classroom to facilitate active involvement and maximize student attention and accessibility to information. On the other hand, student response and student motivation adaptations are means that provide opportunities for students with special needs to demonstrate learning, progress towards meeting the outcomes, and confidence in learning.

What these categories imply is that there are activities or strategies a teacher can employ to adjust, modify, or enrich to meet the learning needs of special needs and English language students. A teacher can restructure, reorganize, refocus, or amplify his or her students' preparation for the lesson to be presented. Some examples of **instructional presentation adaptations** are activating prior knowledge; building background knowledge of content; relating to personal experiences; previewing information; using advance organizers; preteaching vocabulary; using K-W-L strategies, and questioning strategies; activating recall; summarizing; outlining; using cue cards and a vocabulary glossary; simplifying abstract concepts; employing dramatization, music, and guest speakers; interactive writing; drawing or painting; utilizing journal entries; encouraging student "think-alouds"; using self-monitoring checklists; and many others. Some examples of **classroom organization adaptations** are peer partners, cooperative learning groups, physical room arrangement, seating arrangements or seat assignments, lighting, material accessibility, work space, prompting and gesturing, and many other classroom adaptive equipment and materials such as lapboards, personal computers, enlarged print, maps, and others. Some examples of **student response adaptations** that relate to response format and response procedures are information organizers; data charts; illustrations through posters, collages, or murals; journal entries, songs, poems, and raps; bulletin board displays, extended time, practice exercises, use of an interpreter, shorter or more frequent assessments; and many others. Some examples of **student motivation** are creating more interest, activity choice, personally meaningful activities, doable tasks, choice to work with others, student involvement in assessment activities, and many other activities that foster confidence and comfort.

MAKING ADAPTATION: STANDARDS, GOALS, AND SEQUENCE OF ACTIVITIES

In this practical adaptation guideline that we offer, there is a conscious effort on the part of the preservice or inservice teachers to be explicit in the academic content standards that their lesson or instructional plan is covering, specific learning goals addressing the standards, sequence of activities, and ways of monitoring student progress. The adaptation activities are also divided into before, during, and after sections of the lesson. Teacher's instructional strategies are the set of activities a teacher does that focuses on input presentation and the adaptations that include instructional presentation and classroom organization. Student activities are the set of activities students do that emphasizes student response and student motivation adaptations. Figure 2.2 shows a sample set of practice activities in making adaptations:

I.   Selecting a story, topic, or event for the lesson: Read the story "_____" and create a sequence of ADAPTATION activities that you will do to use the story to teach _____ (subject matter/content area)

II. Selecting an appropriate and relevant standards for the lesson: Pick out two or three academic content **standards:**

_____

_____

_____

III. Establishing appropriate and relevant objectives for the lesson: Establish **learning goals** or objectives that are connected to the standards:

_____

_____

IV. Sequence of adaptation activities:

Teacher's Instructional Strategies	Student Activities
Start-up activities: (Before reading) (Preteaching)	
Engagement activities: (During reading) (During teaching)	
Enrichment activities: (After reading) (Postteaching)	

How will you monitor your student progress (objective measures and/or subjective measures): Are they progressing adequately? Do you need to adjust how you are teaching? Do you need to reteach any key concepts? Can the class move forward to a new unit of study?

The sequence of activities for making adaptation includes the selection of appropriate and relevant subject-matter content standards, academic learning goals, teacher's instructional strategies (what teachers do), student activities (what students do), and monitoring of student progress. As you can see in this adaptation sequence of events, **teacher reflection** on what you know about your students and the academic content curriculum; your own pedagogical skills, abilities, and dispositions; categories of appropriate adaptations; and how you will manage instruction and monitor students' progress all play an important role in your purposeful and intentional instructional decisions.

CHAPTER SUMMARY

We have established a case for making academic content adaptation as an equity solution by presenting it as a conscious decision-making process that involves a deep understanding of the societal factors that influence academic achievement and the dynamic interplay among the teacher, the student, and the classroom context in the learning process. "Learning about the students" is a very involved process of figuring out what the students can and cannot do and their level of comfort in recognizing their individuality, working with others, problem solving, demonstrating knowledge, and reflecting on their own learning. It is essential that we also recognize the powerful influence of the "ethic of caring" in driving the teachers' commitment to their students and their learning, respect for their well-being, and advocacy to meet their instructional needs. We hope to provide all teachers with a tool that they can use in making the academic content accessible to all learners.

REFERENCES

Adams, M., Bell, L., & Griffin, P. (Eds.). (1997). *Teaching for diversity and social justice.* New York: Routledge.

Ashton, P. (1984). Teacher efficacy: A motivational paradigm for effective teacher education. *Journal of Teacher Education, 35*(5), 28–32.

Barone, D. (2006). *Narrowing the literacy gap: What works in high-poverty schools.* New York: The Guilford Press.

Bell, L. (1997). Theoretical foundations for social justice education. In M. Adams., L. Bell, & P. Griffin (Eds.), *Teaching for diversity and social justice.* New York: Routledge.

Bemak, F., & Chung, R. (2005, February). Advocacy as a critical role for urban school counselors: Working toward equity and social justice. *ASCA Professional School Counseling,* 196–202.

Brooks, J., & Thompson, E. (2005, September). Social justice in the classroom. *Educational Leadership,* 48–52.

Brown, K. (2004). Leadership for social justice and equity: Weaving a transformative framework and pedagogy. *Educational Administration Quarterly, 40*(1), 77–108.

Cochran-Smith, M. (2000). Blind vision: Unlearning racism in teacher education. *Harvard Educational Review, 70*(2), 157–190.

Cochran-Smith, M. (2004). *Walking the road: Race, diversity, and social justice.* New York: Teachers College Press.

Coelho, E. (2004). *Adding English: A guide to teaching in multilingual classrooms.* Don Mills, Ontario, Canada: Pippin Publishing.

Collier, M. (2005). An ethic of caring: The fuel for high teacher efficacy. *The Urban Review, 37*(4), 351–359.

Cuban, L., & Usdan, M. (Eds.). (2003). *Powerful reforms with shallow roots: Improving America's urban schools.* New York: Teachers College Press, Columbia University.

Darling-Hammond, L., & Baratz-Snowden, J. (Eds.). (2005). *A good teacher in every classroom: Preparing the highly qualified teachers our children deserve.* San Francisco, CA: Jossey-Bass Publishers.

Darling-Hammond, L., French, J., & Garcia-Lopez, S. (Eds.). (2002*). Learning to teach for social justice.* New York: Teachers College Press.

Darling-Hammond, L., & McLaughlin, M. (1999). Investing in teaching as a learning profession: Policy problems and prospects. In L. Darling-Hammond & G. Sykes (Eds.), *Teaching as the learning profession.* San Francisco, CA: Jossey-Bass Publishers.

Edwards, P. A., & Schmidt, P. R. (2006). Critical race theory: Recognizing the elephant and taking action. *Reading Research Quarterly, 41*(3), 404–415.

Elmore, R. F., & Burney, D. (1999). Investing in teacher learning: Staff development and instructional improvement. In L. Darling-Hammond & G. Sykes (Eds.), *Teaching as the learning profession: Handbook of policy and practice.* San Francisco, CA: Jossey-Bass Publishers.

England, C. (2005). *Divided we fail: Issues of equity in American schools.* Portsmouth, NH: Heinemann.

Gordon, R., Lalas, J., & Mcdermott, J. C. (2006). *Omni-education: A teaching and learning framework for social justice in urban classrooms.* Dubuque, IA: Kendall/Hunt Publishing Company.

Gunning, T. (2005). *Creating literacy instruction for all students* (5th ed.) Boston, MA: Pearson Education, Inc.

Gunning, T. (2006). *Closing the literacy gap.* Boston, MA: Pearson Education, Inc.

Haycock, K., Jerald, C., & Huang, S. (2001, Spring). Closing the gap: Done in a decade. *Thinking K–16.* Washington, D.C.: Education Trust.

Kozol, J. (2005). Confections of apartheid: A stick-and-carrot pedagogy for the children of our inner-city poor. *Phi Delta Kappan, 87*(4), 265–275.

Ladson-Billings, G. (2003). Foreword. In S. Greene & D.D. Abt-Perkins (Eds.), *Making race visible: Literacy research for cultural understanding* (pp. vii–xi). New York: Teachers College Press, Columbia University.

Lee, S. K., & Lalas, J. (Eds.) (2003). *Language, literacy, and academic development for English language learners.* Boston, MA: Pearson Custom Publishing.

Marshall, C., & Oliva, M. (2006). *Leadership for social justice: Making revolutions in education.* Boston, MA: Pearson Allyn & Bacon.

Michelli, N., & Keiser, D. (Eds.). (2005). *Teacher education for democracy and social justice.* New York and London: Routledge.

Moll, L., Amanti, C., Neff, D., & Gonzalez (1992). Funds of knowledge for teaching: Using a qualitative approach to connect homes and classrooms. *Theory into Practice, 31*(2), 132–141.

Moll, L., & Arnot-Hopffer, E. (2005). Sociocultural competence in teacher education. *Journal of Teacher Education, 56*(3), 242–247.

Moll, L., & Gonzalez (2001). *Lesson from research with language-minority. Literacy: A critical sourcebook.* Boston, MA: Bedford/St. Martin's.

Nieto, S. (2000). *Affirming diversity: The sociopolitical context of multicultural education.* NY: Longman.

Nieto, S. (2003). *What keeps teachers going?* New York: Teachers College Press.

Noddings, N. (1992). *The challenge to care in schools.* New York: Teachers College Press, Columbia University.

Noguera, P. (2005). The racial achievement gap: How can we assure an equity outcomes? In L. Johnson, M. Finn, & R. Lewis (Eds.), *Urban education with an attitude.* Albany: NY: State University of New York Press.

Popham, W. J. (2004). *America's "failing" schools: How parents and teachers can cope with No Child Left Behind.* New York: RoutledgeFalmer.

Portes, P. (2005). *Dismantling educational inequality: A cultural-historical approach to closing the achievement gap.* New York: Peter Lang.

Rhodes, R., Ochoa, S., & Ortiz S. (2005). *Assessing culturally and linguistically diverse students: A practical guide.* New York: The Guilford Press.

Rodgers, C. R. (2006). "The turning of one's soul"—learning to teach for social justice: The Putney Graduate School of Teacher Education. *Teachers College Record, 108*(7), 1266–1295.

Ruddell, R., & Unrau, N. (2004). Reading as a meaning-construction process: The reader, the text, and the teacher. In R. Ruddell & N. Unrau (Eds.), *Theoretical models and processes of reading.* Newark, DE: International Reading Association.

Schon, D. A. (1983). *The reflective practitioner: How professionals think in action.* New York: Basic Books.

Schon, D. A. (1987). *Educating the reflective practitioner.* San Francisco, CA: Jossey-Bass Publishers.

Singham, M. (2003). The achievement gap: Myths and reality. *Phi Delta Kappan, 84*, 586–591.

Solomon, M., Lalas, J., & Franklin, C. (2006, Spring). Making instructional adaptations for English learners in the mainstream classroom: Is it good enough? *Multicultural Education.*

Stanton-Salazar, R. (2001). *Manufacturing hope and despair.* NY: Teachers College, Columbia University.

Tremmel, R. (1993). Zen and the art of reflective practice in teacher education. *Harvard Educational Review, 63*(4).

Trueba, E. (1999). *Latinos unidos: From cultural diversity to the politics of solidarity.* New York: Rowman & Littlefield Publishers.

Valenzuela, A. (1999). *Subtractive schooling: U.S.-Mexican youth and the politics of caring.* Albany, NY: State University of New York Press.

Young, T. A., & Hadaway, N. L. (Eds.). (2006). *Supporting the literacy development of English learners: Increasing success in all classrooms.* Newark, DE: International Reading Association.

C H A P T E R

Mainstream Teachers Making Instructional Adaptations for English Language Learners and Special Needs Students

In the preceding chapters we have discussed how it has become the concern of mainstream teachers to make instructional adaptations for ELLs and SNSs. This chapter intends to demonstrate the application of the **what, why, and how** elements of making instructional adaptations in mainstream classrooms for the English language and special needs learners. Two studies done on teachers making instructional adaptations will be discussed in detail here. The first study involved a sample of 150 preservice teachers who demonstrated instructional adaptations for ELLs and SNSs, and the second study involved a selected sample of inservice teachers making instructional adaptations for these learners in their mainstream classrooms. The adaptation activities implemented by the preservice and inservice teachers in our samples reinforced our view that these intentional efforts to help ELLs and SNSs require not only content and pedagogical knowledge but also certain dispositions of caring and the ability to teach for equity and educational justice.

This chapter also introduces the notion of teaching performance assessment (TPA), a set of performance-based tasks that is used to determine teacher competence in teaching. Included in the TPA is the task of making instructional adaptations to facilitate learning and obtain access to academic subject-matter content. Including a brief discussion of TPA provides the context for the essential role that making adaptation plays in assessing teacher competence.

TEACHING PERFORMANCE ASSESSMENT: STANDARDS, EXPECTATIONS, ASPECTS OF TEACHING, TASKS

Our interest in the area of making instructional adaptations commenced with our involvement in the assessment of performance of beginning teachers. In the State of California, we have given our implied trust to the California Standards for Teaching Profession (CSTP) in preparing teachers as a way of improving student achievement. Educators and policymakers in California recognize the diversity of students they are serving and the critical need for teachers who are sensitive and responsive to the cultural, linguistic, and socioeconomic backgrounds of all students. To have a common language that will reflect the vision of the complexity of teaching and learning and enable teachers to define and develop their practice, a set of standards that represent a developmental, holistic view of teaching is created. These standards are intended to meet the needs of the culturally, linguistically, and socioeconomically diverse teachers and students in California. The six standards are:

1. engaging and supporting all students in learning,
2. creating and maintaining effective environments for student learning,
3. understanding and organizing subject matter for student learning,
4. planning instruction and designing learning experiences for all students,
5. assessing student learning, and
6. developing as a professional educator.

Teaching Performance Expectations

Applied to the California context of preparing teachers, a more specific list of teaching performance expectations (TPEs) was created. These TPEs are imbedded, categorized, and organized into six CSTP domains. Table 3.1 shows the 13 teaching performance expectations (TPEs) organized into 6 CSTP domains:

TABLE 3.1   Teaching Performance Expectations

CSTP 1 Making Subject Matter Comprehensible to Students
    TPE 1—Specific pedagogical skills for subject matter instruction
CSTP 2 Assessing Student Learning
    TPE 2—Monitor student learning during instruction
    TPE 3—Interpretation and use of instruments
CSTP 3 Engaging and Supporting Students in Learning
    TPE 4—Making content accessible
    TPE 5—Student engagement
    TPE 6—Developmentally appropriate teaching practices
    TPE 7—Teaching English learners
CSTP 4 Planning Instruction and Designing Learning Experiences for Students
    TPE 8—Learning about students
    TPE 9—Instructional planning
CSTP 5 Creating and Maintaining Effective Environments for Student Learning
    TPE 10—Instructional time
    TPE 11—Social environment
CSTP 6 Developing as a Professional Educator
    TPE 12—Professional, legal, and ethical obligations
    TPE 13—Professional growth

Many teacher preparation programs in California require their multiple- and single-subject preliminary credential candidates to pass the TPA before they are recommended for a preliminary teaching credential. The TPA is imbedded in the coursework and linked to California's state-adopted academic content standards.

The California Commission on Teacher Credentialing (CCTC), with the assistance of the Educational Testing Service (ETS) and California educators, developed the California Teaching Performance Assessment (CATPA) through rigorous research, pilot testing, benchmarking, and scoring calibration. The CATPA reflects the set of knowledge, skills, and abilities that beginning teachers should be able to demonstrate before earning their preliminary teaching credential.

Aspects of Teaching

The California Teaching Performance Assessment is created to measure *aspects* of the teaching performance expectations (TPEs) that beginning teachers should know and be able to demonstrate. Table 3.2 outlines the aspects of the teaching performance expectations (TPEs):

TABLE 3.2 Aspects of Teaching

a) Establishing goals/standards (GS)—establishes goals for student learning based on state-adopted academic content standards for students

b) Learning about students (LAS)—learns about his or her students and uses this information to plan instruction

c) Describing classroom environment (CE)—establishes a climate for learning and uses instructional time

d) Planning for instruction (PFI)—uses information about students, strategies, and activities for instructional planning

e) Making adaptations (MA)—adapts strategies and activities for instructional planning

f) Using subject-specific pedagogical skills (PS)—knows and plans to teach the K–12 state-adopted content standards for students

g) Analyzing evidence of student learning and effectiveness of lesson (AESL)—obtains and analyzes evidence of student learning and analyzes the lesson

h) Reflecting (R)—reflects on connecting learning about students to instructional planning

Preponderance of evidence of the teacher candidate's ability to show these aspects of teaching can be gleaned from the candidate's responses and demonstration of practice in performance assessment tasks that are assigned to him or her.

Teaching Performance Assessment (TPA) Tasks

The CATPA tasks have been designed to measure aspects of the TPEs or aspects of teaching such as the GS (goals/standards), LAS (learning about students), CE (classroom environment), PFI (planning for instruction), MA (making adaptations), PS (pedagogical skills), AESL (analyzing evidence of student learning), and R (reflection). The four tasks are shown in Table 3.3.

TABLE 3.3   Teaching Performance Assessment Tasks

Task 1:   Principles of Content-Specific and Developmentally Appropriate Pedagogy
    Candidates will demonstrate knowledge of principles of content-specific pedagogy and developmentally appropriate pedagogy in English/Language Arts, Mathematics, Science, and Social Studies by responding in writing to given classroom teaching scenarios. Candidates will also address assessment practices, adaptation of content for English learners, and adaptation of content for students with special needs.

Task 2:   Connecting Instructional Planning to Student Characteristics for Academic Learning
    Candidates will demonstrate ability to learn important details about a classroom of students, an English learner, and a student who presents a different instructional challenge and plan instruction according to student characteristics by submitting a written response to given prompts.

Task 3: Classroom Assessment of Academic Learning Goals
    Candidates will demonstrate ability to select a unit of study and plan standards-based, developmentally appropriate student assessment activities for a group of students. They will also demonstrate ability to assess and diagnose student learning from responses to the assessment task using assessment instruments.

Task 4: Academic Lesson Design, Implementation, and Reflection After Instruction
    Candidates will demonstrate ability to design a lesson, make adaptations for an English learner and a student with special needs, analyze evidence of student learning, and reflect upon instruction. Candidates will submit completed responses to questions, a videotape of the lesson taught, instructional artifacts, and samples of student work.

As you can gather from Table 3.3, TPA task 1 assesses PS, PFI, PFA (planning for assessment), and MA. TPA task 2 assesses GS, LAS, PFI, MA, PS, and R. TPA task 3 measures GS, PFA, LAS, MA, ASEA (analyzing student evidence and assessment), and R. TPA task 4 measures all eight aspects of teaching such as the GS, LAS, CE, PFI, MA, PS, AESL, and R. All TPA tasks require preservice teachers to make adaptations for the English language and special needs learners.

CATEGORIES OF INSTRUCTIONAL ADAPTATIONS ATTEMPTED BY PRESERVICE TEACHERS

It is clear that one of the essential areas of teaching that is given attention is the set of knowledge, skill, and ability to adapt instruction to meet the needs of all learners, including the ELLs and SNSs, in mainstream classrooms. Here preservice teachers are expected to demonstrate pedagogical skills that include adaptations to accommodate the learning needs of these special learners. Data for our discussion comes from the responses of preservice teachers on TPA tasks that include instructional planning and teaching. Using the New Jersey World Languages Curriculum Framework (1999), the adaptations preservice teachers made in their instructional planning and teaching for ELLs and SNSs are categorized into three areas—(1) Classroom Organization, (2) Instructional Presentation, and (3) Activating Student Motivation and Response. The adaptations related to student response and student motivation are combined into one category to reflect focus on student involvement.

CLASSROOM ORGANIZATION ADAPTATIONS

In order to meet the needs that arise in the learning context for the special learners under consideration, teachers need to make specific adaptations to facilitate their active learning. The major purpose of adaptations **classroom organization** is to "maximize student attention, participation, independence, mobility and comfort; to promote peer and adult communication and interaction; and to provide accessibility to information, materials and equipment." (New Jersey World Languages Curriculum Framework, 1999, p. 200). **Classroom organization** adaptations include organizing instruction with considerations to the special needs of the learners, providing instructional support, and organizing the environmental conditions conducive to learning by providing adaptive equipment and materials. Some examples of classroom organization adaptations are: cooperative learning groups, seating arrangements, cross-age tutors, buddy systems, material accessibility, and many other adaptive equipment and materials such as lapboards, enlarged print, communication board, and other cultural objects.

INSTRUCTIONAL PRESENTATION

Looking at the adaptations of teachers for ELLs and SNSs, it becomes clear what they must do in their instructional delivery to allow accommodations for their special learners. **Instructional presentation adaptations** help special learners to acquire, comprehend, recall, and apply the concepts, ideas, and materials taught. In addition to adaptations, teachers must help students to pay attention to the instruction. In order to do that teachers must make adaptations in their instructional preparation first, then in the methods and prompts they use to teach their content and processes. The next aspect of instructional presentation is the instructional application adaptations that focus on attainment of the instructional goals. In order to achieve this goal, teachers can make adaptations such as activating of prior knowledge, using visual illustrations, and using advance organizers during instruction. Finally, in the instructional presentation monitoring student progress becomes an essential feature. Mainstream teachers must not neglect this area of instruction while dealing with ELLs and SNSs. They must have an ongoing evaluation of student learning, which requires some adaptations in their instructional management.

ACTIVATING STUDENT MOTIVATION AND RESPONSE

Teachers who plan and execute motivation strategies while providing instruction experience success in their teaching. In this category of instructional adaptation, we are encouraging teachers to activate student motivation because students with learning and physical needs are reluctant to fully participate in the learning process of the mainstream classroom due to difficulties they face. We believe that when teachers deliberately make adaptations with specific motivation strategies, they can get students engaged in learning and keep their interest at maximum level. Some of the motivation strategies that can be adapted are providing choice in assignments, hands-on activities, activities that meet various learning styles, and goal setting for learning. Teachers who adapt such strategies in their instruction not only create interest for learning but also confidence in students' ability to learn. An affective strategy validates the students' cultural ways and makes them feel integrated.

Instructional adaptations for ELLs and SNSs also can be made with the anticipated learner response teachers have in mind while teaching. For example, if a middle school science teacher is teaching a science concept and wants the special learners to process the ideas, she or he can have them draw diagrams to demonstrate their understanding. They can also complete a graphic organizer to demonstrate understanding of the concept. The main purpose of planning adaptations for these learners is to monitor the students' progress toward meeting the instructional outcomes of the lesson. When teachers think of this step in the instructional process they are able to think through the teaching and learning sequence that occurs in every lesson. Table 3.4 presents the strategies for the three categories of adaptation preservice teachers in our study made for English language learners.

The list of adaptations our preservice teachers made under each of the listed categories represented their efforts in making learning more meaningful and productive for ELLs. Peer assistance or assigning the student to another student who had bilingual proficiency topped the list under **classroom organization**. In addition, providing learning support through tutoring and paraprofessional assistance was very common in their responses. These adaptations certainly are very practical and doable in the mainstream classrooms. However, this is just a start for making adaptations to accommodate ELLs in their mainstream classrooms. An overall point in the **classroom organization adaptation** is the teachers' special efforts to make the second-language learners feel as part of the class by validating their present academic levels and supporting them to strive further with additional help.

The accommodations preservice teachers made categorized as **instructional presentation adaptations** show the efforts they took to make difficult information meaningful. In general, teachers use various methods to teach content to the different levels of language proficiency of ELLs to provide them access to academic content. Preservice teachers in our program recognized the difficulties ELLs will encounter in their instructional contexts and opted for various types of adaptations to deliver their content. For example, using visual aids, providing a vocabulary list in Spanish, and allowing the ELLs to draw pictures to illustrate their learning were excellent instructional techniques. Although these adaptations are useful steps, further studies have to be done to find out how effective such adaptations really are in cognitively engaging the ELLs to acquire the content meaningfully.

Similarly, modeling as an **instructional presentation adaptation** is an excellent instructional tool, providing an opportunity for the ELLs to visualize what needs to be learned and how it could be accomplished. Modeling as an instructional technique allows the teacher to become an active role model to explicitly demonstrate to students how to learn something or what needs to be learned. It is also a useful strategy in guiding students in reading of a text and comprehending it while rehearsing the mental operations involved in comprehending a selected text. Some preservice teachers in our sample stated they would model learning certain concepts, while others said they would model the process for learning certain concepts. For example, if an experiment has to be conducted to understand a science concept the teacher would model not only the procedures but also the expectations of the experiment. In these contexts, modeling would serve as an excellent tool for ELLs to understand content concepts and provide both

TABLE 3.4   Types of Adaptation Strategies for English Language Learners

Classroom Organization	Instructional Presentation	Activating Student Motivation and Response
• After school/before school tutoring	• Preteach and reteach	• Include the EL in student presentations to encourage the development of confidence and oral and language skills
• Work one on one in class when time is available	• Make learning goals specific	• Accept oral answers vs. written answers
• Provide additional time	• Focus on content and meaning instead of grammar and spelling in the written work	• Use dialogue and other forms of oral expression to process content ideas and concepts
• EL paraprofessional assistance for one-on-one instruction	• The assessment stresses vocabulary	• Write directions on the board
• Sit with a translator	• Daily journals	• Allow ELLs to do research in Spanish
• Elicit parental support and cooperation	• Modeling	• Student draws a picture to illustrate her learning and her thoughts
• Place the ELL closer to the teacher to make sure the materials are clear and directions are heard	• Graphic organizers	• Student rewrites rules and explain them in own words
• Recognize cultural characteristics and validate them—such as the accent and ways of interaction	• Bubble cluster	• Allow student to finish a written report with pictures to represent the learning
• Pre-lesson assignment	• KWL chart	• Provide guided practice
	• Provide Spanish vocabulary list	• Portfolio to record student learning and monitor progress
	• Vocabulary wall in English	• Make adjustment in the assessment cueing to the student's level of understanding
	• Use illustrations to teach science concepts	• Alternative assignment
	• Include English development standards in the content	• Personally meaningful group work
	• In an assignment that requires written description, the ELL just labels the pictures orally	• Omit singling out in front of class
	• Slow down the pace of teaching to accommodate the ELL	• Reduce number of paragraph to a few sentences
	• Make adjustments in journaling activities	• Reduce writing requirement
	• Provide visuals and examples before and during lesson	• Provide glossary of words taken from the content to be discussed ahead of time
		• Show samples of assignments—a simple paragraph
		• Reduce writing requirement
		• Less quantity in assignment
		• Peer tutoring
		• Pair with bilingual student
		• Assign homework before and after a lesson
		• Provide positive feedback on written or spoken answers
		• Teacher as editing service
		• Translated materials
		• Modified assignments in writing
		• Positive feedback

academic and linguistic cues. This method should be studied further as to how its application would assist ELLs in the learning of content knowledge in mainstream classrooms.

Our preservice teachers made additional adaptations that fall under the category of **activating student motivation and response.** These adaptations relate to what students have to demonstrate in response to the instructional context and are directly connected to the curriculum and its delivery for understanding content. For example, making learning goals specific, using translated materials, and modifying assignments are constructive efforts to make the learning content relevant and appropriate for the ELLs. However, in order to provide opportunities for meaningful learning, other types of adaptations are needed. For example, "focus on content and meaning instead of grammar and spelling in the written work" is a great start, but providing instruction that enables meaningful knowledge acquisition involves further actions. Making adaptations of materials at the ELL's reading levels in English, increasing efforts to develop comprehension of content materials, and grounding their learning through effective vocabulary instruction and prior knowledge activation would be excellent strategies. Such adaptations would not only meet their linguistic needs but also keep their motivation high in the learning process.

The adaptations listed here for ELLs are good strategies teachers can use, but these alone will not be sufficient. The teachers must establish a context-rich learning environment to allow opportunities for ELLs to negotiate meaning of the content. For example, adaptations such as after/before-school support, working with another expert student or a bilingual aide, group work, and peer tutoring are practical instructional accommodations that might help. They certainly provide opportunities for the ELL to receive feedback about his or her understanding of the material to be learned or the learning activity that must be completed. Similarly, using translated materials, giving modified assignments, and reteaching are examples of curriculum accommodations made by the mainstream teacher for the ELL to have access to content. While these strategies provide opportunities for academic access and engagement, we must remind teachers that it is very difficult to gauge how successful these adaptations are in the mastery of academic content. In order to achieve language development and content learning, teachers need to demonstrate high expectations for their English language learners, strong understanding of language learning, effective pedagogy, and consistent reliance on good assessment data to guide instruction (Linquanti, 2004).

Relevant, appropriate, and effective instructional adaptations must eventually bring the ELLs to actively engage in negotiating meaning of the learning context and demonstrate achievement of academic goals. That can be done by amplifying and enriching the language of the classroom, using new words in context and paraphrasing that context, employing instructional scaffolding and schema building, and using assessments that inform student progress. Such accommodations would provide rich learning opportunities that allow the ELLs to weave new information presented in the class into structures of meaning or schema that exist in their learning systems.

MAKING ADAPTATIONS FOR SPECIAL NEEDS LEARNERS

In the case of making instructional adaptations for special needs students (SNS), it should be pointed out that their needs are widely different. Moreover, the individual educational plan (IEP) process considers the instructional manageability of the students before they are transitioned into the mainstream classrooms. Therefore, mainstreamed SNSs in most cases have the basic learning skills, so teachers usually deal with them as their regular "at-risk" learners. Preservice teachers' responses were based on the type of SNSs they had selected for focus. The special needs learners these teachers selected represent a wide range of disabilities, and that makes it very difficult to present the adaptations in a general format. Readers must be aware that some of the adaptations shown in Table 3.5 correspond to a specific disability. Nonetheless, the listed adaptations can be organized within the framework in Table 3.2 in the same way as the data on ELL learners.

CLASSROOM ORGANIZATION ADAPTATIONS

The listed adaptations here concern establishing a supportive learning environment for the special needs learners. Grouping students of similar learning characteristics was a major adaptation these teachers made. Other efforts indicate using existing resources within the system such as instructional aides, special education teachers, and the IEP team. Those accommodations would work together in various ways to provide the emotional and academic support these learners need. Making special technical adaptations for students with severe speech and visual handicaps is also essential. The overall emphasis of these adaptations is the awareness, knowledge, skills, and abilities of mainstream teachers in making special efforts to create a learning atmosphere that takes into consideration the special physical, emotional, and academic needs of SNSs.

INSTRUCTIONAL PRESENTATION ADAPTATIONS

In making adaptations for special needs learners, our preservice teachers did not make any compromise in teaching the grade-level content standards they were required to teach. However, they made special efforts to simplify the content materials to their special learners' academic levels and innate learning difficulties. They made adjustments in the amount of materials as well as in the learning expectation levels. They added special materials and manipulatives to teach difficult concepts. They modeled learning ideas and used visuals to present content. One notable adaptation here is making adjustment in the learning expectations demonstrated through writing. They were willing to settle for oral responses from students who could not demonstrate content mastery through writing. Although all of these **instructional presentation adaptations** assist in all students' learning, they have special implications for SNSs.

ACTIVATING STUDENT MOTIVATION AND RESPONSE

In making adaptations to activate student motivation and response, our teacher candidates showed great concern. They recommended different ways that students could complete

TABLE 3.5   Types of Adaptations for Special Needs Learners

Classroom Organization	Instructional Presentation	Activating Student Motivation and Response
• Ability grouping • Small-group activities • Team with parents • Provide small-group instruction • Provide adult assistance through aides • Seated in front • Work individually • Partner with regular students • Work with a partner scaffolding the tasks	• Include assessment in the learning content • Differentiate the learning tasks • Give writing tasks at a lower grade level • Use many visuals • Use observation log to document student learning behavior • Use manipulatives in math, reading, and writing • Use many hands-on activities • Chunk the content with expository materials • Use graphic organizers to teach concepts and ideas • Use oral assessment for part of the test and rest with the whole group • Modeling and using visuals • Student does paired reading with a fluent reader • Make adjustment in the writing expectations • Do modeling of read-alouds • Use computer as an alternative resource • Shorten the amount of guided practice and help work independently • Provide alternative rubrics • Make shared reading adaptation • Provide vocabulary on flash cards • Give fewer comprehension and analysis questions • Closely monitor all phases of the lesson while handling students with behavior problems • Monitor the progress student is making in comprehension of content materials • Provide individual assistance to clarify vocabulary and finding meaning of key words	• Different mode and venue for providing responses to questions • Avoid verbal responses for students with speech difficulties • Students write journal entries • More time given for transitioning from one task to another • Use simple worksheet • Work individually to help with learning tasks that are not completed • Provide opportunities to redo assignments • Repeat assessment till mastery is achieved • Provide adapted resources such as reteaching a worksheet and giving extra time to finish work • Use observation log • Have student listen to texts on CD • Do shared reading with oral retelling followed by writing • During silent reading time sit with the student and have him read to the teacher • Assess after instructing for reaching content standards and see what assistance is needed; provide assisstance • Allow to write assignment on note cards rather than paper • Preteach the day before and give questions to answer • Attend the IEP meeting and have a connection with parents • Send weekly progress notes home • Use a pair of silencing headphones for ADD learners • Send additional work home to improve deficit areas of learning

assignments. They used various methods to teach the content, allowing the special learners to process it within their limited functioning levels. They recognized time on task as a vital element in learning by allowing extra time to learn, providing special assistance to learn, and modifying the academic content materials. The adaptations listed here show that our preservice teachers made special considerations for engaging the SNSs in the learning process in their classrooms.

INSTRUCTIONAL ADAPTATIONS BY INSERVICE TEACHERS

Teaching has become a blend of whole-class, small-group, and individual instruction requiring teachers to be "flexible in their approach to teaching and adjusting the curriculum and presentation of information to learners" (Hall, 2002, p. 2). This implies that teachers no longer can develop one standard lesson plan and teach it. In order to teach all students effectively, mainstream teachers have to develop a frame of mind that includes multiple options for not only teaching information but also for making sense of ideas and mastering the delivered knowledge. They have to develop varied adapted instructional approaches in relation to individual and diverse students in their classrooms. In other words, instead of getting frustrated with the differences prevalent in the classroom and expecting students to be at grade-appropriate readiness level, the time has come for teachers to adapt their instruction for diverse students in the classroom.

The teachers in our study exemplify the type of adaptations we are recommending for mainstream teachers to develop for ELLs and SNSs. Our teachers were trained in the adaptation process, format, and procedures that we have developed. This process begins with the teachers learning about their students and paying special attention to the cultural and educational background of ELLs and SNSs. Then, the teacher plans the instruction for three distinct learning phases, making adaptations in each phase The three phases are preteaching or start-up activities, engagement activities that take place during the lesson, and enrichment activities that take place at the end of the lesson. If teachers organize their instructional planning and delivery around these phases, it becomes easier to make the needed adaptations for special learners. Our sample teachers made special efforts to learn about their students, paying specific attention to cultural and academic factors of the ELLs and SNSs. They documented what they learned about them and used that information as a precursor to planning instruction. Then, they infused the different adaptations into the start up, engagement, and enrichment phases of the lesson. At the end of the instructional adaptation process, our inservice teachers shared their personal reflection on the significance of making adaptation for their ELLs and SNSs.

In the next section, three of our sample teachers from elementary and secondary schools will be discussed in detail, showing how they made instructional adaptations for their English language and special needs learners. Each teacher will be presented as a case with a brief description of the teacher's background, training, and philosophy of teaching. Then, their instructional plans showing adaptations for ELLs and SNSs will be described. Finally, their reflections on how their instructional adaptations worked will be presented.

THERESA

In the past 17 years as an early-grade teacher, Theresa has been trying to continually hone her teaching skills. Learning about the teaching practice has been an ongoing process since getting her teaching degree and credentials. She remembers vividly her first day of teaching in Tiffany Elementary as a second-grade teacher. It was much different from what she sees in her classroom in terms of the kind of students she has now. At present, 70% of students in her school are ELLs, and there is great racial diversity in her classroom. Through all the changes she has seen and is seeing, Theresa's teaching philosophy continues to move toward becoming more inclusive. "I believe all children should have equal opportunity to learn whether in small groups or individually. Students all learn differently," she said delightfully. She makes sure that her teaching style becomes versatile to meet the various needs of her students. In addition, Theresa values the background knowledge of each of her students and takes that into consideration when she plans instruction. She also makes sure to know what type of skills each of her students has and provides enrichment opportunities for those who lack basic learning skills.

As part of the sample teachers in our study, she first did the preassessment step by collecting information about her special learners to learn about their backgrounds and school experiences before taking steps to make deliberate adaptations for ELLs and SNSs. Theresa saw significant results not only in their learning behaviors but also in her teaching. She said, "I have really changed, especially after teaching the units I developed for this study. My ELLs were excited to participate in the class because I had already pretaught the vocabulary and prepared their minds for the lesson. They felt confident to answer questions during the lesson and some even kept raising their hands before others." She adds, "I continue to slow down when the English language and special needs learners are in the whole group and point out key words when we read and discuss lessons." After seeing the success of her instructional adaptations, Theresa vows to carry on this new teaching tradition she has developed for her practice. Figure 3.1 shows one of Theresa's lessons with the numerous adaptations she made for the special learners in her classroom.

Social Studies Standards K–2: 1.2 Students compare and contrast the absolute and relative locations of places and people and describe physical and/or human characteristics of places.

Language Arts Standards: 2.4—Use context to resolve ambiguities about word and sentence meanings. 3.2—Describe the roles of authors and illustrators and their contributions to print materials. 3.3—Recollect, talk, and write about books read during the school year.

Written and Oral English Language Conventions: 1.1—Write and speak in complete, coherent sentences.

Learning Goals: 1. Students will locate the United States, North America, and Europe on a map and globe. 2. Students will identify folktales they know.

Thematic Unit: Cinderella

(Continued)

Figure 3.1 Theresa's instructional adaptations: Sequence of adaptation activities.

Preteaching Adaptation: Start-up Activities

Adaptations for ELLs: 1. Explain what folktales are. Provide examples of some they may be familiar with. 2. Explain that Cinderella is a type of a folktale called a fairytale 3. Explain what a fairytale is. 4. Introduce the vocabulary from the story. In addition, explain what stepmothers and stepsisters are, as well as princes and fairy godmothers. Show the characters from the book and prepare the students for reading the story.

Adaptations for Special Needs Learners: 1. Explain what folktales are. Provide some they ma be familiar with. 2. Explain that Cinderella is a type of a folktale called a fairytale 3. Review the important elements of the story. 4. Review vocabulary that will be critical to the other stories.

During-Teaching Adaptation: Engagement Activities

1. Introduce the unit to the class and then the European Cinderella story. Explain that it is a very old folktale called a fairytale. Name other fairytales the students are familiar with. 2. Explain what stepmothers and stepsisters are, as well as princes, fairy godmothers, and balls. Explain the elements of a fairytale. Use the illustrations from the book. 3. Have students share what they know about Cinderella. 4. Using a bubble map, list what students know about Cinderella. 5. Explain to students that the Cinderella they are familiar with originated in Europe many years ago and that other countries also have a type of Cinderella story, but they use customs in their culture. Explain that we will be hearing these stories from different countries.

During-Teaching Adaptation: Engagement Activities for ELLs

1. Have students sit near the front.

2. Look at students when the vocabulary appears in the story and read the sentence again.

3. Read the story slowly.

4. When possible, simplify the language.

During-Teaching Adaptation: Engagement Activities for SNSs

1. Have students sit in front.

2. Look at the students and make sure they are repeating the vocabulary words and sentences.

3. Provide an incentive for being involved in the discussion, for example, have them point to the vocabulary words or point to the illustrations. Or have them help hold the book.

After-Teaching or Beyond-Lesson Adaptation: Enrichment Activities: Students do a graph of a favorite story of their selection.

After-Teaching or Beyond-Lesson Adaptation: Enrichment Activities for ELLs: 1. Have students draw a picture of a character or a scene from the story 2. Have them retell the story to the teacher 3. Keep vocabulary words from the unit in a pocket chart and have students review the words and their meanings as illustrated on the cards 4. Provide a list of words for the students to keep in their pocket book, which is a place where students keep the activities they complete.

After-Teaching or Beyond-Lesson Adaptation: Enrichment Activities for SNSs

1. Write the story in their own words and pictures. 2. Fill in a column on a matrix developed for the story. 3. Keep the vocabulary words in their pocket chart.

Figure 3.1 Theresa's instructional adaptations: Sequence of adaptation activities (Continued).

Teacher Reflection

Theresa's reflection on her experience of making instructional adaptations for her special learners and her thoughts about teaching all learners are very positive. Here is an excerpt from her reflection journal:

> "Making instructional adaptations for my ELL and special needs learners has been a great experience for me. Chunking the instructional period into three phases has been very helpful. Preteaching the lessons and vocabulary while other students were working on other assignments has been useful. I reviewed five words that would be in the story every time. The information I found about my ELL and SNS certainly helped to recognize their learning difficulties and also understand the differing emotional components of the students. While the other students were working on another assignment I pretaught the lesson and the vocabulary to my ELLs first and then to SNSs. That helped the learners to be continuously engaged in the lesson while I taught. Then, as part of the extension activities, I worked with these students in small groups to complete their extension activities while the rest of the class worked on their own. I have also instructed my special learners to sit in close proximity to me during the whole lesson . . . During the year these students had difficulty focusing during whole-class instruction. Yet, when I worked with them in a small group, they were completely different children. They were interested, engaged, shared their thoughts and ideas, and felt special because they were with their teacher. They also seemed to grasp the material more easily . . . they were also more attentive, excited, and focused than they ever were during the year . . . Moreover, by providing the students with a preteaching lesson, I was able to give them two opportunities to learn the information. This was a successful adaptation where the students were also able to feel the experience of success . . . I was thrilled to witness how much more attentive, engaged, and focused these students had become during whole-class lessons. Since they felt success in a small-group setting, they weren't afraid to share their answers or ideas with rest of their peers. Working individually on the extension activity also enabled them to orally share with me what they learned and eased some of the pressure of having to do it on their own . . ."

At the conclusion of her reflection Theresa states, "I would definitely recommend preteaching and working individually with ELL and students who have special needs. Working in small groups before and after the lesson also provided an opportunity to clear up misconceptions they may have acquired. The practice not only benefited the students, but also me. I was able to practice what I was going to teach on these students. If they didn't understand it, I was able to rethink how to explain a word or concept differently."

ANITA

Anita, a "new generation" teacher, certainly fits the picture of the teacher of the new millennium. She is broadminded and tolerant in her outlook and has fashioned a classroom that suits her ideals. When she began teaching in the San Bernardino schools as a fourth-grade teacher she learned that diversity is here to stay and that she had to become inclusive in her approach to teaching and living. When asked about her philosophy of teaching she went on to say, "My philosophy is that all students can learn. I believe dealing with diverse students is a challenge that can be tackled when all aspects of learning are taken into account: the teacher, the student, and the classroom environment. I believe that when a teacher acknowledges and values students' diverse backgrounds and abilities, he/she sends a clear message that says, I care about who you are and I value your beliefs."

Making her classroom a safe place for diverse students is Anita's priority and she works very diligently in creating a classroom that supports student differences. Learning about her special learners when the year began helped her to understand their different cultural and home backgrounds. She was also able to determine their academic levels and recognize their learning needs. That is why Anita makes her classroom the starting point at which each student will be helped to work toward his or her full potential. In addition, she uses students' interests, personalities, and backgrounds to create lessons that best suit individual students. In spite of the limited resources in the school, she works hard to make her classroom a resourceful learning place for all learners. The following is a sample lesson from Anita that includes teaching and learning adaptations for ELLs and special needs learners.

Content Standards on Vocabulary and Concept Development: Apply knowledge of word origins, derivations, synonyms, antonyms, and idioms to determine the meaning of words and phrases.

Learning Goal: Students will generate synonyms for new vocabulary words in order to gain a clear understanding of word meanings, and then use this knowledge to generate sentences using the vocabulary words.

Preteaching Adaptation: Start-up Activities for ELLs

1. Before the lesson write the vocabulary words on index cards and use the pocket chart to display one word at a time and teach the ELLs—**sprightly, strides, rhythm, stammers, clutching, determined, steady, and sweltering.**

2. Explain to students that they will be learning some new words that will help them understand the main character in a new story they will be reading as well as increase their personal vocabulary knowledge.

3. In a pocket chart display only one word at a time and pantomime each word.

4. Show a picture that represents the word and discuss the picture and more meanings or synonyms.

5. Have them generate words from homes that represent the vocabulary words.

Preteaching Adaptation: Start-up Activities for SNSs

1. In a small group have them read the vocabulary words and show pictures to illustrate each word.

2. Build confidence in their ability to recognize the words in a text.

3. Discuss the meaning of each word, even by pantomiming.

4. Prepare them to read the words in the text.

(Continued)

Figure 3.2 Anita's instructional adaptations: sequence of adaptation activities (Continued).

During-Teaching Adaptation: Engagement Activities: During whole-class instruction, include the special learners and see how they connect with the classroom discussion and activities. As each vocabulary word is taught, the story with the vocabulary word in the text is introduced. The class reads the story and the teacher shows the context for each of the words selected.

During-Teaching Adaptation: Engagement Activities for ELLs

1. Pair them with an advanced learner who will assist in following the lesson.
2. While the vocabulary words are identified in the text, make special eye contact with them to show how the word fits the story, highlighting the meaning of the selected words.
3. Discuss how the words were helpful in understanding the story.
4. Have them find the words in the text and underline them with a pencil.
5. Provide them sentence strips made with the vocabulary words highlighted and synonyms written separately in small cards.
6. Show them the list of vocabulary words with the synonyms next to each word.

During-Teaching Adaptation: Engagement Adaptations for SNSs

1. Place them in small groups with other learners.
2. As whole-class instruction is going on, have an eye on them to make sure they are working with others in doing the activities.
3. Have them find the vocabulary words in the text and underline them.
4. Replace the vocabulary words with the synonyms on the given sheet.
5. Provide the vocabulary list with the synonyms.

After-Teaching or Beyond-Lesson Adaptation: Enrichment Activities: Students generate their own sentences using the vocabulary words.

After-Teaching or Beyond-Lesson Adaptation: Enrichment Activities for ELLs

1. Have them copy the sentences with the vocabulary words.
2. Have them copy their sentences with vocabulary words replaced by the synonyms.

After-Teaching or Beyond-Lesson Adaptation: Enrichment Activities for SNSs

1. Have them copy the sentences with the vocabulary words.
2. Have them copy their sentences with vocabulary words replaced by the synonyms.

Figure 3.2 Anita's instructional adaptations: sequence of adaptation activities (Continued).

Teacher Reflection

Anita's reflection specifically speaks about how the activities she designed before, during, and after reading fit with the process of teaching vocabulary. It is supported by the theory of the meaning construction process proposed by Rudell and Unrau (2000). She provided English language and special needs learners and others with background knowledge in the hopes of providing motivation for engagement and touching on their sociocultural values, which enhances the affective conditions of the reader. She also attempted to develop their knowledge of language by enhancing schema and lexical word knowledge. Here is an excerpt from her reflection:

> "The ELLs and SNSs in my class had low academic skills and lacked the confidence to participate in class activities. Getting them to be part of the whole class was the first challenge I had to work on. These students lack critical thinking skills and reflective thinking skills. Knowing this, I created an adaptation lesson where the students would not have to talk too much at first. I included pantomime at first to engage students and then followed with the use of visual pictures to get them thinking about what the words might mean. With this safety net, we only discussed the words briefly. I then made a home-school connection by having the students generate words from homes that represent the vocabulary words. They were excited to do this. Once I had a good understanding of my ELL and SNS's backgrounds, I grouped them according to ability and their personalities. Then I created adaptations based on their abilities, their characteristics, and their strengths.
>
> Some of the difficulties I faced came from not being creative enough to get them to open up. I wasn't sure if the pantomime was causing confusion and reluctance. First I pantomimed the words, then the regular students came up with synonyms as these special learners watched what was going on. Then I used pictures to show the words in action in the real world. This was much more tangible for them and gave them an extra-clear understanding of the words. It was a bit time consuming, but the results were worth it."

VALESCA

Teaching for 29 years has not made Valesca in any sense a traditional teacher with "old" ways of teaching. She is indeed a teacher with many insights and a large bag of teaching "tricks." Her classroom is an active place where students fully engage in the learning of science content. Having learned English as a second language and having become an American citizen have made her a special kind of a teacher who is able to meet the learning challenges of ELLs and SNSs. She has become a symbol of a teacher for the modern times because of her cultural and language backgrounds, which are assets to teaching students with many differences. Her teaching philosophy is based on a motivation theory. She says, "My focus on teaching is to motivate my students to learn. I use hands-on teaching methods and try to reach all kids in my class . . . .There is no one way to teach; you have to show variation in methods." Her instruction is often inquiry-based and requires students to use their critical skills to think about their learning. "Engaging students in the learning process is the biggest thing to do in teaching," says Valesca. When asked how she engages all learners, she replied, "Using my best teaching practices; besides, I'm bilingual—making adaptations is not difficult for me."

In her middle school classroom she has a large number of SNSs in one of her periods and a set of ELLs in another hour. She learns about her students before they even come to her class. She goes through the school records to read about her special learners first and makes notes on the needs they might face. Since she is bilingual, teaching science for second-language learners is not a big problem for Valesca. Her adaptations are different for each of those instructional periods because of the high concentration of each of the groups. For example, in one period 24 of the 36 students she has are special needs learners, and in the other 17 of the 34 students are ELLs. The following lesson plan shows the type of adaptations she made for the science lesson on the topic "Acids and Bases in Chemistry."

Content Standards: Grade 8

Concept 5: Chemical reactions are processes in which atoms are arranged into different combinations of molecules. As a basis for understanding this concept: **Standard a.** Students know reactant atoms and molecules interact to form products with different chemical properties. **b.** Students know the idea of atoms explains the conservation of matter: In chemical reactions the number of atoms stays the same no matter how they are arranged, so their total mass stays the same. **c.** Students know how to determine whether a solution is acidic, basic, or neutral.

Objectives: 1. Students will understand the differences about acids and bases, lab test how various forms of acids and bases are found in commonly used items, and understand methods of distinguishing acids from bases. **2.** Students also will see that cabbage juice turns colors in different everyday chemicals, and it identifies the chemical as an acid, base, or neutral. Students will make predictions and then test their predictions.

Teacher Instructional Activities

Preteaching Adaptation: Start-up Activities for ELLs

- Provide the vocabulary list made up of words from the lesson to look up in the dictionary a day ahead of time.
- Provide picture illustrations for difficult words.
- Read the chapter ahead of time.

Preteaching Adaptation: Start-up Activities for SNSs

- Read the chapter ahead of time.
- Write down the main ideas on a given concept map graphic organizer.

During-Teaching Adaptation: Engagement Activities:

- Through a series of engaging activities students will form a functional definition of acids, bases, and neutrals.

Engagement Adaptations for ELLs

- I will use manipulatives, drawings, posters, tables, and props to illustrate the concepts.
- I will use hand motions to help them understand the lessons being presented. I will also use real-life examples of elements discussed.
- I will also use group work for others and have ELLs work in pairs so that I can monitor the learning.

Engagement Adaptations for SNSs

- I will use manipulatives and graphic organizers.
- I will also have them work in groups to do processing activities.

(Continued)

Figure 3.3   Valesca's instructional adaptations: Sequence of adaptation activities.

After-Teaching or Beyond-Lesson Adaptation: Enrichment Activities:
Enrichment Adaptations for ELLs: In the lab work, pair the ELL with a student who knows the language or someone who is helpful.
Enrichment Adaptations for SNSs: In the lab, work in small groups.

Figure 3.3   Valesca's instructional adaptations: Sequence of adaptation activities (Continued).

Teacher Reflection

Valesca likes to reflect on her teaching because it allows her to see if she reinforces her teaching philosophy. As a middle school science teacher, she strives to engage her learners in the learning process, and all the changes that are going on in today's understanding of education have influenced her to make her classroom a place for exploration and experimentation. Being a science teacher, she tries hard to develop critical thinking in her students, always engaging them through project-based learning. The following excerpt from her reflection shows her passion and commitment to making academic success for all her learners achievable:

> "My ELL and SNS learners seemed to have done well this morning. They were able to do all the activities, including the lab-related activities. Providing the vocabulary words before the day of teaching that content definitely helped. Making adaptations for them has become a day-to-day thing for me. The lesson organization I have followed has helped me greatly to plan engaging work for all learners. I really believe in the strength of the constructivism approach of integrating different learning styles. This is the basis for making adaptations for my ELL and special resource students in the mainstream science class. I implement exercises that will engage students in more comprehensive ways and that will take into consideration their different learning styles, which I believe is the best way to teach. I also use cooperative group settings, which allows me to integrate social and cultural groups and their varying performance levels . . . By constantly making adaptations to ensure my students are engaged during the main teaching phase, I make sure that the material is clear for them. I believe that by being a bilingual teacher with much enthusiasm for teaching, I am able to be patient with my students' learning difficulties."

These three teachers demonstrated resiliency and endurance in their professional practice through the instructional adaptations they made for their special learners. The more adaptations they made, the better the results they observed in the performance of their students. This confirmed to others that being tolerant of learning differences and exercising patience in helping diverse learners overcome their learning difficulties is a successful strategy. Teachers like these are the trailblazers for changing the teaching and learning culture of our schools.

CHAPTER SUMMARY

It must be emphasized here that asking mainstream teachers to make instructional adaptations for ELLs and SNSs is only the first step and not an end by itself. Other steps are needed to create a learning culture that takes into consideration all the factors related to learning English for academic success and providing the needed support for the special education students. Seeing preservice teachers taking the lead in this matter is very encouraging. The teacher training institutions are certainly on the right track toward reaching their mission of training teachers to possess knowledge, skills, and abilities in making adaptations as equitable instructional solutions. However, that is not enough because the veteran teachers also must join others in bringing equity in the learning process for all learners, which implies that teaching innovations such as instructional adaptations cannot be done by just a few. A portrait of a school that has equity as its core will show equitable learning conditions, a collaborative teaching and learning system, supportive intercultural school structures, and individuals with a transformative spirit.

REFERENCES

Cummins, J. (1986). Empowering minority students: A framework for intervention. *Harvard Education Review, 15*, 18–36.

Cummins, J (1996). *Negotiating identities: Education for empowerment in a diverse society.* Los Angeles, CA: California Association for Bilingual Education.

Deschenes, C., & Sprague, J. (1994). *Adapting curriculum and instruction in inclusive classrooms: A teacher's desk reference.*

Echevarria, J., Vogt, M., & Short, D. J. (2000). *Making content comprehensible for English language learners.* Needham Heights, MA: Allyn & Bacon.

Gandara, P. (2005). U.S.Davis News & Information. U Service, 530-752-1.

Garcia, G., & Beltran, D. (Ed.). (2003). *Reaching the highest level of English literacy.* International Reading Association.

Hall, T. (2002) *Differentiated instruction.* Wakefield, MA: National Center on Accessing the General Curriculum.

Haycock, K. (1998). Good teaching matters: How well-qualified teachers can close the gap. *Thinking K–16, 3*, 1–2.

Haycock, K., Jerald, C., & Huang, S. (2001, Spring). Closing the gap: Done in a decade. *Thinking K–16.* Washington, DC: Education Trust.

Leyba, C. (Ed.). (1994). *Schooling and language minority students: A theoretical framework.* Sacramento, CA: California State Department of Education.

Linquanti, R. (2004). A framework for teaching English learners. *R & D Alert*, a publication of West Ed., vol. 6, No. 3.

Miller, P., & Endo, H. (2004). Understanding and meeting the needs of ESL students. *Phi Delta Kappan, 85*, 786–791.

New Jersey World Language Curriculum Framework. (1999, Winter).

Reyes, M. (1992). Challenging venerable assumptions. *Harvard Educational Review, 62*(4), 427–446.

Roe, B. et al. (2004). *Secondary school literacy instruction: The content areas* (8th ed.). Boston, MA: Houghton Mifflin Company.

Rumberger, R., & Gandara, P. (2004). Seeking equity in the education of California's English Learners. *Teachers College Record, 106*(10).

Short, D. (1991, Fall). Integrating language and content instruction: Strategies and techniques. NCELA Program Information Guide Series, Number 7.

C H A P T E R

Adaptable Literacy Strategies and Technology Support Resources for All Students

Jose Lalas, Margaret Solomon, and Gary Stiler

The sources of materials, strategies, and technology support for making instructional adaptations abound for all students, including English language learners and special needs students. Making instructional adaptations, as we have learned from previous chapters, is a deliberate, cognitive, and practical process that involves a teacher's conscious reflection of who his or her students are, what appropriate and relevant concepts to be taught, why the students are doing the assignments, why the concepts and processes being covered are significant, and how the adaptation will be carried out to benefit the target students. This chapter will present practical teaching ideas and technology support resources appropriate for literacy and language development.

We support our ideas and discussions on a variety of literacy issues by including a comprehensive review of key studies in reading and writing and giving practical examples for clarity. Preservice and inservice teachers will find these literacy strategies and technology resources helpful to them in making academic content instructional adaptations for the English language and special needs learners.

READING ASPECT OF LITERACY

What do we know about reading? We already know that reading is a multilevel, interactive process. More than two decades ago, Spiro, Bruce, and Brewer made this conclusion in their study of the nature of reading. They asserted that

Reading is a multilevel interactive process; that is, text must be analyzed at various levels, with units of analysis going from the letter to the text as a whole. In addition to processing the explicit features of text, the reader must bring considerable preexisting knowledge to the reading comprehension process. The interaction of text-based and knowledge- based processes and of levels within each is essential to reading comprehension. Because the meaning of text is only partially determined by the text itself, reading must be an inferential, constructive process, characterized by the formation and testing of hypotheses or models about what the text is "about," a process similar in many ways to problem solving. (1980, p. 3)

Currently, this characterization of the reading process continues to influence the field (Blair-Larsen & Williams, 1999; Combs, 2002; Tompkins, 2007) and implies that reading is facilitated by one's ability to process text information using background knowledge and language proficiency from the integration of text-based-level and knowledge-level processes. It means that as a reader decodes, he or she uses his or her background knowledge and language ability to understand what is on the printed page. We all know that a student who does not speak, understand, read, or write English cannot read and comprehend English! As a beginning reader or beginning language learner of English, he or she may look at the print, the letter, the word, and the sentence but at the same time use his or her background knowledge, skills, and abilities to understand what is on the page. In this view of how reading occurs, it is believed that children learn to read by having a balanced exposure to " skills and meaning bearing language accesses" with letter-sound, word parts, and words on the decoding end and sentences and discourse on the comprehension end of a developmental framework (Shuy, 1983). Thus, children learn word recognition skills while they become proficient in reading comprehension.

BALANCING WORD-CENTERED SKILLS AND MEANING-CENTERED STRATEGIES

We offer in Figure 4.1 the conceptual framework for balancing the word recognition skills and meaning-centered strategies in instruction for English language learners and special needs students.

It can be seen from Figure 4.1 that word-centered skills include sight words, phonics, syllabication, morphemic analysis, and context. Sight words are words that occur with high frequency, such as *the, a, of, at, them, to, in, is*, and *be*, and are learned through visual memorization. Phonics consists of knowledge of the relationships between letters and sounds and the ability to discriminate, categorize, blend, segment, and manipulate sounds represented by letters. Syllabication is a word analysis technique that breaks words into smaller parts to assist a reader in pronouncing the parts and blending them into familiar words. Morphemic analysis is a word-attack skill that examines a word to locate and derive the meanings of the morphemes, the smallest units of meaning; in using morphemic analysis, one can determine a word's meaning through examination of its prefix, root, and/or suffix. Context use is an attempt to derive the meaning of a word by examining the context that precedes the word or by looking at the words and sentences that follow it. All these skills are focused on word recognition and analysis.

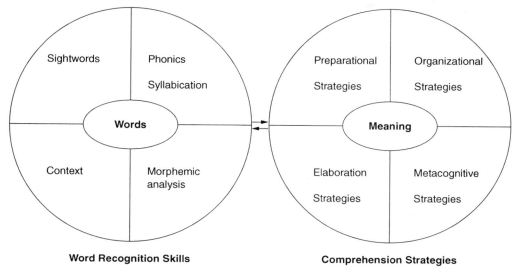

Figure 4.1   Balancing skills and stategies: A conceptual framework.

One of the word-centered skills that has been clearly connected to initiating and promoting literacy in countless empirical studies is phonological awareness (Bryant & Goswami, 1987; Perfetti, Beck, Bell, & Hughes, 1988; Wagner, Torgesen, & Rashotte, 1994). It is the consciousness that a spoken word is composed of a sequence of speech sounds. (The sound units in phonological awareness include syllables, parts of syllables, onsets and rimes, and phonemes; the sound units in phonemic awareness are phonemes). Durgunoglu, Nagy, and Hancin-Batt (1993), in their study of children who were native speakers of Spanish and were learning English as a second language, found that phonological awareness and word recognition in Spanish predicted word recognition in English and significant correlations and influences between phonological awareness and word recognition across languages. Bialystok (2002) viewed the findings of Durgunoglu, Nagy, and Hancin-Batt's rigorous study as important because they demonstrated that the phonological awareness skills developed in one language transferred to reading ability in another language. He concluded that "if children can establish basic concepts of phonological awareness in any language, then reading will be facilitated irrespective of the language in which initial literacy instruction occurs" (p. 186).

The following section provides examples of phonological and phonemic awareness activities (Ehri & Nunes, 2002).

Phonological Awareness Tasks

- Rhyming words: given a spoken word, student can produce another word that rhymes.
- Onset-rime segmentation/blending: given a single-syllable spoken word, student can segment it into its onset (any consonants, digraphs, or blends preceding the vowel) and rime (vowel and following consonants, e.g., "dog" into "d" - "og," "chop" into "ch" - "op,"

"stop" into "st" - "op"). Given spoken onset and rime, students can blend them to form a word.

- Syllable segmentation/blending: given a spoken word, student can segment it into syllables; given spoken syllables, students can blend them to form a word.

Phonemic Awareness Tasks

- Phoneme isolation: given a spoken word, student can isolate and identify the first sound; the final sound.
- Phoneme identity: given spoken words "bike" "bell" and "ball," student can identify the sound that is the same.
- Phoneme blending: given phonemes spoken separately, student can blend the sequence to form a word; process involved in decoding written words.
- Phoneme segmentation: given a spoken word, student can break it into its phonemes; process needed to invent spellings of words.
- Phoneme deletion: given a spoken word such as "smile," student can remove "s" and say what remains, "mile."
- Phoneme oddity: given three or four words, student can identify the one that does not belong because it lacks a phoneme present in the other words (e.g., *bus, bun, rug*).

Figure 4.1 also shows four strategies that are meaning-centered. Gunning (2005) names four major comprehension strategies: preparational strategies, organizational strategies, elaboration strategies, and metacognitive strategies. **Preparational strategies** include activating prior knowledge about a topic before reading, predicting what events will happen in the story, setting purposes and goals for reading, and previewing the content of the text or story. **Organizational strategies** are conscious steps employed during as well as after reading in comprehending the main idea and the important details, organizing details in the passage, sequencing events and procedures, and summarizing. **Elaboration strategies** are meaning-centered activities during as well as after reading in which the reader constructs connections between information from text and prior knowledge by making inferences, forming images, generating questions, and evaluating the content of the text. **Metacognitive strategies,** as in Chamot and O'Malley's Cognitive Academic Language Learning Approach (1996), include checking for comprehension during reading, planning how to accomplish the task by outlining or identifying the organizing principle, reading selectively by attending to key words, ideas, or information, and reflecting on what is learned. The following are Anderson and Roit's (1996) 10 instructional suggestions that have been proven effective in promoting language and literacy development for English language learners:

1. Shared reading: involves a teacher reading and sharing a book with students.
2. Vocabulary networking: often called semantic webbing or mapping.
3. Expanding contexts: after clarifying a word, students can discuss what it has to do with the selection, other selections, or their own experiences; could be accomplished by asking a simple and consistently phrased question, such as "What does this have to do with the rest of the text?"

4. Predicting: it is important that students first talk about their understandings of story segments or pictures before they try to predict from them.

5. Imagery: visualizing or creating a mental image of something in a text; one way to encourage imagery in reading is to talk more about illustrations.

6. Text structures: organizational options that authors utilize when producing texts; studies have shown that teaching text structures to language minority students increases their comprehension.

7. Questioning, identifying problems, and sharing strategies: all students need to feel free to ask questions, tell others about problems they are having, and share and evaluate ideas for solving those problems.

8. Explaining text: asking students to retell; students should always be encouraged to try to explain what the text means and to discuss and compare their explanations with other students.

9. Culturally familiar informational texts: could activate students' prior knowledge; provide an opportunity for language minority students to demonstrate their intelligence by discussing their own experiences and providing new knowledge to their peers.

10. Conversational opportunities: students must be provided with ample opportunities to practice English with a native speaker on a conversational basis, to exchange information and to find out about language in a friendly, enjoyable, and unintimidating way.

IMPLICATIONS FOR ENGLISH LANGUAGE LEARNERS AND SPECIAL NEEDS STUDENTS

English language learners (ELL), in the context of public education in the United States, are students who speak English as a nonnative language. Those who are just beginning to learn English or are in the intermediate level of using English are often referred to as limited-English-proficient students (LEPs). Oftentimes, these students are also called second-language learners, English-as-a-second-language students, and English learners. The challenge facing the school system is how to teach these English language learners (ELLs) English and how to read in English as a second language. On the other hand, special needs students (SNSs) are those students who have a learning "disability" that can be caused by a weakness in the information processing system that may include visual-perceptual skills, attention span, motor skills, and auditory processing and language skills. They often experience problems with basic decoding skills due to lack of phonemic awareness and automaticity in processing printed information (Gunning, 2005). Both the English language and special needs learners need ample opportunities to apply their skills in reading materials that are relatively easy for them to read and understand in a very caring and supportive environment.

Current research in second-language acquisition tells us that the degree of children's native-language proficiency is a strong predictor of the rapidity of their English language development (August & Hakuta, 1997). This means that the more knowledge of reading and literacy one has in his or her first language, the better off he or she will be in a second language.

It is common knowledge now that the ability to read in one's first or native language transfers in learning to read in a second language (August & Hakuta, 1997; Baker, 1996; Minami & Kennedy, 1998). Consequently, students who are not able to read and write in their first language are the most challenged in learning how to read in English as a second language.

While some researchers support the delay in formal reading instruction until ELLs have a reasonable command of English (Snow, Burns, & Griffin, 1998; Wong-Filmore & Valadez, 1986), many believe that reading instruction and oral language development in English as a second language can be simultaneously provided with positive consequences (Anderson & Roit, 1996; Goodman, Goodman, & Flores, 1979). Bialystok (2002) explained that "bilingualism might be a necessary condition for the efficient development of advanced literacy, but it is not a sufficient condition. The local effects are governed by the structure of specific languages and writing systems, the exposure to instruction in literacy, and the cognitive baggage invoked by the task used to measure the skill" (p. 192). Bialystok included in her extensive review studies on the acquisition of literacy by bilingual or partially bilingual children in a weak language, such as the experience of Hispanic children in the United States who acquire English language literacy in school in spite of having weak command of spoken English. She reported that children in this category typically achieve lower levels of reading competence than do their peers and require between 4 and 7 years to reach grade-level standards in academic and literacy achievement.

According to the Individuals with Disabilities Education Act (IDEA), *specific learning disability* means "a disorder in one or more of the basic psychological processes involved in understanding or in using language, spoken or written, which may manifest itself in an imperfect ability to listen, think, speak, read, write, spell, or to do mathematical calculations." It has been found that about 80% of special needs students classified as learning disabled have a reading difficulty. Because of the special needs students' lack of decoding skills and their tendency to read below grade level, they need high-interest reading materials in a caring, print-rich classroom.

COMPOSING ASPECT OF LITERACY

There is a growing knowledge base on writing and writing instruction that we can use to enrich our teaching of writing to all students, including English language and special needs learners.

We now know that writing is a complex productive process that involves cognition and memory. A writer encodes messages in a manner that reflects his or her intentions, background knowledge, and target audience. Dahl and Farnan (1998) explained that writing can be defined "as composing and expressing ideas through letters, words, art, or media and print, something that only occurs when mental operations (processes) are mobilized for the purpose of composing and expressing ideas" (p. 5). Current research studies and textbooks clearly explain that this "writing process" consists of prewriting, drafting, revising, editing, and publishing (Hughey & Slack, 2001; Tompkins, 2006). This popular description of the writing process developed from early process-observational studies on writing that characterized the process as recursive as well as linear. For example, the seminal study on composing conducted by Emig (1971) delineated the different observed components of the composing process such as the context of composing, nature of stimulus, prewriting, planning, starting, composing aloud, reformulations, stopping, contemplation of product, and seeming teacher influence. Emig explained that students in high school were not given enough prewriting activities and enough opportunity for revision.

In another earlier study conducted by Flower and Hayes (1977, 1980), writing process was viewed as a problem-solving process. They explained that writers do not dutifully plan, generate, and construct in that order but "thought in writing moves in a series of non-linear jumps from one problem and procedure to another" (Flower Hayes, 1977, p. 460). They found that the difference between good writers and poor writers was how the elements in the rhetorical problem were given attention. Rhetorical problem means the different elements writers actively take into account as they write, such as the assignment, audience, and the writer's own goals in involving the reader, persona or self, meaning, and text. Good writers seemed to respond to all aspects of the rhetorical problem more than the poor writers. They considered not only their audience and assignment thoroughly, but also their goals of involving the audience, their own persona, and the text. Poor writers, on the other hand, seemed to be primarily concerned with the features and conventions of the text, such as number of pages or format.

Bridwell (1980) demonstrated in her study the association between the students' levels of revision and the quality of their writing. Good writers showed revision at the sentence and multisentence levels. Poor writers revised very little, typically at surface and word levels, merely recopying their first drafts, and gave too much attention to hundreds of spelling and punctuation changes while writing.

Composing in the Primary, Intermediate, and Middle School Grades

Early studies on children's composing gave us insights on how writing occurs. Graves's early studies (1975, 1979) of 7-year-old and 6-year-old children's writing revealed that children seemed to follow the steps of prewriting, writing, and revision. Based on this research, Graves explains that when children write they choose topics from their own experiences, write narratives more than other forms, and discover meaning while they write because they think and play on paper. While some children rehearse through drawing and other creative forms and talk before and during writing, others rehearse through reading, watching television, or daydreaming and use no overt language to accompany the act of composing.

In another early observational study on young children, Murray (1982) documented writing as a process consisting of prewriting/prevision/rehearsal stage, writing/vision/drafting, and rewriting/revision. He explains that prewriting, which consists of planning, brainstorming, conceptualizing, and other notetaking activities, occupies about 85% of the writer's time while drafting or the production of the first draft occupies only 1% of the writer's time.

Dyson's early study (1983) on the role of oral language in composing revealed that talk provides the meaning and, for some children, the systematic means for getting that meaning on paper. She (1992) also addressed the sociocultural contexts that influence what and how children use cultural information they know from cartoons, movies, video games, and neighborhood observations as elements for writing. In her more recent study, Dyson (2000) explained that it is speech in the form of critical social dialogue that will help student writers understand the literary, social, and political ramifications of their chosen written genres, plots, characters, and words.

Langer's (1986) study of the writing process of intermediate-grade writers shows that in general, intermediate students are aware of the strategies they use to convey their message meaningfully and to make sense of the content about which they are writing. These strategies include generating ideas, formulating meaning, evaluating, and revising. Research on middle school writers shows an increased attention to planning and understanding of genre and text structure. It appears that middle school writers become more careful in addressing the audience, content, genre, and structure in their writing. They work back and forth in their drafts as they consider new options and possibilities based on their understandings of genre, text structure, audience, and content.

Dahl and Farnan (1998) reported that in the primary grades, children view writing as spontaneous play. Children experiment with letters, words, spacing, and other writing materials, and are very eager to communicate their written messages to their peers and teacher. As they become more able writers, they soon realize that they are not always sure of what they have written and that their teacher and classmates have questions about what they write. Although their early writings seem to be spontaneous and unplanned, evidence of rehearsal of ideas through think-aloud and other oral language activities begins to appear. Young primary-grade writers also use their experiences with children's books for themes, character ideas, or story starters for writing their own original works. Intermediate-grade writers, on the other hand, have more self-awareness and write most frequently about personal experiences, personal interests, and a variety of information, including friends, social problems, and imaginary characters.

ADAPTABLE READING-WRITING CONNECTION ACTIVITIES

The following are common practical classroom activities that can be adapted for the English language learners and special needs students:

1. **Reader's Theater:** Script the original story into dialogue for oral presentation. Students can be asked to write the scipt with guidance from the teacher.
2. **Open Mind:** Using the outline of a head, write/illustrate the character's thoughts and feelings. Example of a prompt: If you can get into the mind of the character, what thoughts and feelings are there? Fill in the head picture with symbols, drawings, images, and/or words that represent what the character is feeling or thinking.
3. **Quick Draw:** Students are asked to illustrate a scene from the story before, during, or after reading the story.
4. **Hot Seat:** A student or students is/are to take the persona of a character in the story. The other students interview them for their reactions, thoughts, and feelings in the story.
5. **Journal Writing:** Students write responses to the paragraph, chapter, or story events in their journal. Personal interaction with the reading material is thus fostered.
6. **Venn Diagram:** Students compare/contrast objects, events, or characters in the story.

7. **Graphs:** Students create or attempt to understand visual organizers (e.g., matrix, Venn diagram, thermometer, web).

8. **Story Sequencing:** Students order the events of a story.

9. **Story Writing:** Students retell the story through writing.

10. **Story Mapping:** Students create an actual map of the events in the story.

11. **Interview:** Invite a guest from the same cultural background or similar experience of the book.

12. **Poetry:** Haiku, cinquain, copy change, for example; can reflect the setting, character, or theme of the book.

13. **Create a Dictionary:** Make a dictionary of the book's vocabulary.

14. **Choral Reading:** Teacher asks the students to read the story together.

15. **Questioning:** Ask/write questions about the story/character. Teacher models how to ask using the different levels of comprehension questions—literal, inferential, critical, etc.

16. **Cover Predictions:** Ask questions—Who is this person? What is this book about?

17. **Talk Show:** Interview the character as a talk show host.

18. **Write Your Own Ending:** Students are asked to think and come up with their own interesting ending for the story.

19. **Book Jackets:** Students create a jacket for the book they read. They design original illustration on front and write a brief summary on the back.

20. **Make up a Song:** Students rewrite the words to a popular tune/song describing the character, theme, story, setting.

21. **Newspaper:** Students work in a group create a newspaper article or section.

22. **Role-Playing:** Students make up a play retelling the story.

23. **Letter Writing:** Write a letter to the character—asking questions, telling your feelings about the book, giving advice, etc. Students take on the identity of the character and write to a significant person in the character's life.

24. **Slide Show:** Students create a slide show of the events in the story.

25. **Inside/Outside Circle:** Students write things that are the same inside the circle and things that are different outside the circle.

26. **Postcard:** Students create a postcard illustration and write to family/friend as if they had visited the location.

27. **Board Game:** Students create a board game with questions and cards asking questions about the story.

28. **K-W-L-H:** Know, Want to Learn, Learned. The teacher leads the students in filling in the K-W-L-H sections as a class, small cooperative groups, or with a partner.

29. **Comic Book:** Students create a comic strip with dialogue of the main events in the story.

SELECTED CONTENT-AREA AND ACADEMIC LITERACY STRATEGIES

K-W-L-H Chart

The K-W-L-H chart is a commonly used basic technique for relating students' prior knowledge to new information and concepts through reading and writing. This can be used in whole-classroom instruction, with each student writing what they know and what they want to find out about a particular topic or content concept. For example, in a seventh-grade geography class the unique physical features of each continent is the topic. The teacher asks all students to read the text to find out the information and asks them to compare any two continents, listing their differences and similarities in a Venn diagram. Second-language learners in this class may need special assistance in doing this assignment; however, when they complete this activity they will have come across many new words and will have made some cognitive connections to the ideas they present about the selected two continents. Following that activity, as per Anna Uhl Chamot's suggestion, the teacher adds "H" to the chart to ask students to write down "How I learned and what I learned" (Chamot, 1995). This helps students to build awareness of learning strategies that helped them to learn a concept. When students fill those columns they are able to metacognate and establish purpose for learning. Besides, this activity guides students to interpret and extract information from text, compose, and use writing conventions to express their ideas (Cummins, 2001).

EXPLAIN THE REFERENCE WITH CONTEXT

This activity incorporates information read from a text to compose a written response. It is called "explain (in writing) the selected reference with context." After reading a narrative text the teacher underlines a selected portion and asks the student to explain in writing the context of the statement and why it was made. This invokes the student to interpret the information the text brings. For this activity, both narrative and expository texts can be used. When a narrative text is used by the teacher to have students construct meaning through writing, the teacher underlines a statement by a character in a plot of a story and asks student to explain the statement with their own words, substantiating it with events or deeds that highlight the statement. In this activity, the underlined statement in a narrative or expository text encourages the student to think and wonder about what is emphasized in the underlined part of the text and think deeper about the context. Next, the student's explanation in this assignment can be turned into a written account of what happened in the story, providing a learning experience that focuses on a form or use of English language. Similar applications can be made for SNSs also.

TEXT-TO-SELF CONNECTION

Text-to-self connections (Tovani, 2000) is an excellent activity that allows the learner to read parts of a text and make connection to self. After reading a text, either narrative or expository, the teacher models to students by copying a sentence or two from the text and writes down the connections she or he made between the quotations and her or his personal life. Here is a sample sheet for this activity:

Text-to-Self Connections

1. Text
Quote:_____
_____
_____
_____

This reminds me
of. . . _____

    Students can then select one or two sentences that appeal to them and write them down. While they think about those sentences cognitive language development occurs naturally, and when they write down their thoughts in the given space, they read and reread what they wrote. An activity like this certainly would have many challenges for second-language learners who can't understand all the words in the quote; this is when teachers have to provide special assistance, but that should not make them overlook the importance of second-language learners doing this activity with meaning and purpose. The teacher can go one more step with this activity by asking students to do a journal entry of this activity to add further meaning and purpose to the meaning they constructed of the various sentences they copied and made connections to with their prior knowledge. This example again shows how to bring all three strands of academic language development together and provide ample opportunities for students to process meaningful language and concepts.

CONTENT WORD AND IMAGING

This activity (Tovani, 2000) helps in developing deeper meaning with new vocabulary students learn in their content classes. Mainstream teachers with ELLs and SNSs can very effectively use this strategy for the whole class. Before or after reading a text, difficult words are highlighted and explained. Then students are asked to think about the images that come to their mind and draw the pictures. Here is an example of an activity sheet:

Content Words and Imaging

Content Words	**Images that Come to My Mind**

They also write words to express their images. In addition to doing several word-imaging tasks followed by reading, students draw a poster to illustrate several meanings and images they derive from content words. This activity also allows for English learners to deepen their awareness of how various English words can be conceptualized and used.

THE ESSENCE OF THE TEXT

This is another learning activity (Tovani, 2000) based on using content texts to increase the comprehensible input and using the understanding gained in writing to refine their conceptual learning. Here, after teaching a topic from a content text, the teacher selects a particular portion of the text and asks students to read it individually. Then they orally discuss the text, focusing on these three questions: "What was the text about?" "What is essential to remember from the text?" "What is most important in the text?" Students work in groups to answer these questions and discuss them. Once this task is completed, students then write down their answers to those three questions on a sheet similar to the following example. Then they read their answers to their peers and evaluate them for their quality.

What was the text about?
What is essential to remember?
What is most important in the text?

By doing this, English learners are able to retell their understanding through writing and metacognitively process what they learned from the text and differentiate what was essential to remember and what was most important to remember. This learning can end with the students writing a summary paragraph of the text they studied.

Probable Passages: A Reading-Writing Strategy

This activity (Billmeyer & Barton, 1998) can be done mainly with narrative texts. After reading a selected story, the students chart their answers on an activity sheet that has the following components. This allows them to dissect the story and look at it in a critical manner.

Setting	Characters	Problem	Solution	Ending

Students think about the story from the context of the posed problem and its solution and gain an opportunity to think in detail about the setting of the story and how the characters play their roles. This activity can conclude with a further writing assignment asking students to rewrite the story with their own ending to the story. In doing this type of thinking, different aspects of cognition are developed and second-language learners, in that process, learn words and make meaning of the story in various ways.

RAFT

RAFTing (Unrau, 2004) is a great writing and thinking activity that can be used in any content class. This consists of four parts: role, audience, format, and topic. After learning a content concept from a textbook chapter, RAFT can be introduced for students to explore the content through writing in a purposeful manner. First, they select a role they want to play in speaking about their topic and then determine their audience. Then they decide in what form they want to write—a story, speech, advertisement, or other form of writing—then finalize what message they want to deliver, and pursue their writing. This activity can be done as whole-class activity until students become familiar with it. Later it can be used as individual writing activity. This can be a great tool to motivate ELLs and SNSs to think about the content as they write. Here are some examples of RAFTing:

Role	Audience	Format	Topic
Newspaper Editor	Citizens	Editorial	Freedom of Expression
An Artist	Statue of Liberty	Questions	Ideals of Liberty
A Leaf	Plant Kingdom	Story	Chlorophyll

JOURNALS

Journal writing can be used as a method for developing the individual thought processes of students. "Each time teachers ask students to compose in journals, they individualize instruction, forcing passive learners to become actively engaged" (Unrau, 2004, p. 290). Journals certainly engage students in deeper thinking. In the case of ELLs and SNSs journaling can assist in reinforcing learning and stimulating imagination. By writing in the journals they can also clarify their thinking.

TECHNOLOGY APPLICATIONS AND SUPPORT RESOURCES

This section discusses the opportunities associated with using emerging technology to support English language learners and special needs students with cognitive or communicative disabilities. It explores digital access issues and the background of technology-supported language learning and assistive technology. It also looks at contemporary software applications and assistive technology that includes graphic organizer software, image galleries, writing projects, multimedia and streaming video, virtual tours, and forms of real-time communication. Finally an examination of specific forms of emerging technology that includes e-mail, MP3 players, instant messaging, text messaging, chat rooms, and blogs is offered.

The applications presented here are not mutually exclusive to the needs of language learners or special needs students. While some applications may tend to better support the needs of second-language learners, students with communicative or cognitive disorders, for example, may also benefit from technology that promotes literacy development and writing skills.

THE DIGITAL DIVIDE: CONVERGENCE AND ISOLATION

Socioeconomics, age, gender, ethnicity and geography have an effect upon who uses technology (U.S. Department of Commerce, 2002, 2004). Findings from the Pew Internet and American Life Project (Lenhart, Madden, & Hitlin, 2005)indicate that less than 73% of 12- to 17-year-olds from families earning less than $30,000 are Internet users. Those 12- to 17-year-olds who are unplugged from the Internet are more likely to be African American than Hispanic. However, even as Hispanic and African American Internet use is relatively low, members of this group are still more likely to be Internet users than is the majority of American adults (Lenhart et al., 2005, p.1). The Pew Internet and American Life Project also reported that one of the most rapidly growing segments of Internet use is among English-speaking Hispanics.

Internet use is strongest among 12- to 17-year-old users, as 87% of "Millennials" are online, as are 82% of 18- to 24-year-olds ("GenY"). Both groups have a heavy reliance upon Internet-mediated forms of communication that include instant messaging, online gaming, blogging, text messaging, music downloads, and general web searches (Fox & Madden, 2005). Use by gender is also significant. Older girls, ages 15 to 17, are more likely to be engaged in Internet communication and information-seeking activities than are boys of the same age (Lenhart et al., 2005). In an era of decreasing computer prices, Arrison (2002) notes that the digital divide between users and nonusers is narrowing as he cites findings from the U.S. Department of Commerce (2004) that suggest that the gap has become one more of choice than of economics.

When persons with disabilities are included in this analysis, perceptions about a narrowing digital divide change. Issues include computer ownership, access to computers and the Internet, graphic verses text-based web pages, and a lack of accessible hardware design (Kaye, 2000; Waddell, 1999). Kaye (2000, p.10) relates that "within each racial and ethnic group, the rate of computer ownership is much less when there is a disability present in the household than when there is not." While solutions to these issues are emerging, it is apparent that the use of technology cannot be an assumed panacea.

TECHNOLOGY SUPPORT: LANGUAGE LEARNING AND SPECIAL NEEDS

Special needs students have cognitive disabilities in one or several domains. These include

a language, communication, and auditory reception

b reasoning, idea production, and cognitive speed

c memory and learning

d visual perception

e knowledge and achievement (Carroll, 1999, p. 5, cited in Wehmeyer, Smith, & Palmer, 2004).

Contemporary communication and computer-based technology offers platforms for students to practice and engage in meaningful communication that includes oral, written, and graphic interface. It encourages social interaction that can be characterized as synchronous (face-to-face) or asynchronous (e.g., email). As a medium of communication, cell phones, text messaging, and webcams can include content-based topics as well as skill-building exercises. As a metacognitive prompt, the use of communication technology helps students to construct dialogue or text, make inferences, and reflect upon appropriate responses. Finally, as a constructivist teaching strategy the use of these technologies encourages students to explore ideas and make meaningful personal choices.

ENGLISH LANGUAGE LEARNERS

Socially interactive technology (SIT), technology-supported learning (e-learning), and computer-mediated communication (CMC) opportunities appear to enhance student learning (Apple Education, 2002; Bryant, Sanders-Jackson, & Smallwood, 2006; Honey, Culp, & Carrigg, 1999; Kimble, 1999). However, impacts on English language learners are more difficult to ascertain. With the exception of traditional technology-supported second-language-acquisition models (e.g., ESL), adaptations of mainstream technology appear to be the norm, rather than initiatives specifically designed for English language learners. In schools where e-learning designed specifically for ELLs has been used, Svedkauskaite and Reza-Hernandez (2003) reported positive impacts on language learners.

As a model, computer-assisted language learning (CALL) has been around since the 1960s. Bax (2003) described early forms of CALL as *closed systems*, usually language labs, where students were monitored by teachers while they engaged in listen-and-respond activities. Since then, CALL has evolved alongside advances in technology, to emerge as an interactive form of e-learning. Today, CALL is invested in multiple forms of computer-mediated communication that blend both static forms of listen/read-and-respond teaching strategies as well as multimedia and web-based learning. The role of teachers has evolved into one of facilitation and interaction with the advance of new forms of media.

Debate continues as to whether or not contemporary forms of CALL have a significant impact upon second-language acquisition. LeLoup and Ponterio (2003), in a review of literature about the effectiveness of CALL, report several emerging opportunities. They report that:

a   learning activities that permit computer-mediated contact with others tend to produce more language than face-to-face discussions;

b   language production activities are more universal among participants, rather than dominated by a small number of students;

c   student language production is greater; and

d   cultural awareness among participants is increased. (p.2)

These findings coincide with what we know about best practices in second-language pedagogy; that teaching and learning should be contextualized, interactive, multisensory, and metacognitive (Lalas, Solomon, & Stiler, 2005). When this framework is applied to specially designed academic instruction in English (SDAIE), specific strategies emerge. These include the use of graphic organizers, visuals, manipulatives, realia (real objects), and collaborative learning.

How can literacy skills, metacognition, and oral language production be enhanced by technology? Given the disparate experiences and perceptions between teachers and their students, as well as findings about best practices in computer-assisted language learning, it seems appropriate to explore existing and emerging forms of e-learning as they may be applied to second-language acquisition. Potential adaptations and emerging technologies include graphic organizers, image galleries, writing projects, multimedia, virtual field trips, games and quizzes, e-mail, streaming video, text messaging, chat rooms, instant messaging, MP3 players, and blogs. How these may be used to promote English language learning is described in the following section. Associated links for each adaptation can be located among the references.

SPECIAL NEEDS STUDENTS

Assistive technology (AT) has a broad application when applied to classroom uses. Behrmann (1998) discusses the multiple forms and applications AT may take in the classroom and describes them as ranging from "low tech" to "high tech" (p. 75). High-tech applications include software, computers, and other devices. Behrmann extends this definition to include practice tutorials, multimedia, and Internet applications. Other applications include augmentative and alternative communication aides (AAC). Devices include those that support speech, language, and learning disabilities. Products include symbol-making, picture board software (e.g., Boardmaker), speech synthesizers, personal digital assistants (PDA), picture-based e-mail programs, and graphic, voice-enabled web browsers (Braddock, Rizzolo, Thompson, & Bell, 2004; Hawking, 2001).

ADAPTATIONS OF EXISTING/EMERGING E-LEARNING TECHNOLOGIES AND SOFTWARE

Graphic Organizers

Comprehension of ideas and concepts may be facilitated through the use of graphic organizers. SDAIE strategies generally incorporate the use of visual displays and graphic organizers. A graphic organizer is a visual display that depicts the relationships between facts, terms, and or ideas within a learning task. Graphic organizers can also be used by students to illustrate prior knowledge and to illustrate comprehension (Williams & Gomez, 2001). Hall and Strangman (2002, p.1) define graphic organizers as "knowledge maps, concept maps, story maps, cognitive organizers, advance organizers, or concept diagrams." They serve the important purpose of permitting students to design knowledge constructs, maps, and connections (O'Malley & Chamot, 1990).With regard to special needs students, the use of graphic organizers promotes independent reading, content assimilation, and autonomy and becomes a tool that can be used across content areas (Blankenship, Ayers, & Langone, 2005).

Inspiration and *Kidspiration* offer teachers and students opportunities to author unique visual displays (Inspiration Software, 2003). According to the company's research base, the production of displays utilizes incipient metacognitive strategies to enhance reading comprehension and student achievement. While Inspiration is more appropriate to the older learner, Kidspiration has been designed for K–5 students and utilizes audio and visual elements to permit users to design and construct meaningful and personal representations of ideas or concepts.

IMAGE GALLERIES

Visual images are used to elicit prior knowledge and to cue students about planned instruction. As a form of an anticipatory set, visual images or pictures are often used as a prompt. They provide contextual clues that help students to determine meaning. Visual images may connect new learning to prior experiences or place it in a sociocultural context. Pictures are also used to elicit a nonlinguistic response to new concepts (Wallace, 2004).

Even with the best of intentions, teachers have a difficult time locating and archiving the images they need. However, online picture and image galleries contain large numbers of pictures for classroom use. They can be viewed online or downloaded and printed. Options include Google Images (2006), Picture Dictionary (2004), Discovery School Clip Art Gallery (2005), Clip Art for L2 Instruction (2003), Language Teaching Clip Art (n.d.), and Pics4Learning (2002).

WRITING PROJECTS

Writing skills are often some of the more difficult skills to teach. While drill and repetition are important, so is a meaningful writing objective. As students progress through the writing process (prewriting-writing-revising-editing-rewriting), it is important that students also see a purpose for their writing. An example of a meaningful writing project is found at the *Dual Language Showcase* (Chow, 2001). The Thornwood Public School outside of Toronto has a student population representing at least 40 languages and cultural groups (p.1). Elementary-age students write books about themselves, their homes, and their families that are published online as part of the Showcase.

Older students can participate in the Diary Project (2003). The project is a global network that encourages teens to write about topics of the day, or on ongoing discussions covering 24 topics ranging from tolerance to friends, family, and religion. The Diary Project began in 1995 as a reaction to a need for teen dialogue expressed by a young Bosnian writer who wrote about her life in Sarajevo. With respect to user safety issues, Diary Project submissions are previewed and monitored by a team of adults and teens.

A proprietary reading/writing software package called *Wiggleworks* (2006) was developed by Scholastic and the Center for Applied Special Technology (CAST) as a multimedia learning tool for emergent readers. Wiggleworks integrates text, audio, images, and speech as prompts for young readers and writers. As a culminating element of the package, writers rewrite stories in their own words, using images and color to produce unique, personal publications.

MULTIMEDIA, STREAMING VIDEO, VIRTUAL FIELD TRIPS, AND MP3 PLAYERS

Multimedia learning invites learners to use visual, aural, and text-processing skills. While learner preferences may not always correspond with all three modes, vocabulary acquisition is optimized by multimedia support (Chun & Plass, 1996). Multimedia also supports content knowledge construction for limited-English-proficient students and serves as effective models and prompts for special needs students (Mechling, 2005; Svedkauskaite & Reza-Hernandez, 2003). *WebQuests* are one of the most common examples of multimedia use applications. WebQuests are multimedia inquiry tools that promote the exploration of problems, issues, and questions. Well-designed WebQuests engage students in collaborative problem solving as they navigate the Internet in search of answers. Teachers often design or adapt WebQuests to their lessons in ways that support emerging literacy skills, provide important roles for special needs students, and involve learners in multimodal activities. Important WebQuest portals include WebQuest.org (2006) and WebQuests (2000).

Other multimedia adventures give emphasis to the exploration of ideas, places, and history. The Jason Project (2005), as one example, invites students to become co-explorers of contemporary math, science, and technology problems.

Other forms of multimedia teaching tools include *streaming video* and *virtual field trips*. Popular streaming video providers include United Streaming (2005), Power Media (2006), and Digital Media (2005). Streaming media offer students the opportunity to explore exotic, familiar, and unfamiliar environments. Video clips can be used to capture the attention of students, provide models, enhance lessons, and to evoke emotional responses and dialogue among viewers (Brooks-Young, 2005). Instructor-created videos for special needs classrooms effectively promote behavior change and skill acquisition among students (Mechling, 2005; Mechling, Ghast, & Langone, 2002).

Virtual field trips can take students from the middle school in a nearby town to the great museums of the world. The Utah Education Network (2005) manages *Virtual Field Trips*. This online tool permits teachers to design and create field trips to their own school or across content topics ranging from science and health to fine arts and math. Virtual Visits (2004) takes visitors on shopping trips and to historic sites as they learn about contemporary issues and career opportunities. Thinkport's (2006) online field trips "provide rich, interactive multimedia content including interactive stories, maps, games, timelines, audio." (p. 1). Online trips include science and math discoveries, art, literature, and history.

Self-guide walking tours can now be downloaded and archived to portable devices. MP3 players have the capability to store and play more than music. They can take students on tours of museums, play back lectures and voice recordings, tune into radio stations, and serve as platforms for student-made radio shows called *podcasts*. Podcasting is an Internet-based MP3 application gaining widespread popularity among adolescents and young adults as a personal broadcast medium (Lalas et al., 2005). Users design, script, and broadcast audio programs. In much the same way as traditional radio broadcasts, podcasts are designed to contain information or entertainment targeting general or specific audiences. Podcasts may be of short or long duration, and contain dialogue, narrative, and music. Well-designed programs maximize creativity, cross-disciplinary connections, and collaboration among developers. Good podcast programs are dependent upon the development of strong academic literacy skills exemplified by a well-written script that attracts and retains listeners. Important elements include clarity of narrative, cogency of argument, humor, and integrity.

Games and Puzzles

Coinciding with Millennials' attraction to emerging technologies is their fascination with games. Entertainment is no longer the sole function of computer games. Interactive peer-to-peer games occur as a combination of entertainment and learning activity. This merger is often referred to as *edutainment*. To Millennials, simulations can serve as entertainment or as *serious games* (SG). Prensky (2005) noted that Millennials prefer complex games that present significant challenges to users. Social impact games and interpersonal simulations require higher-level thinking and problem-solving skills (Gamest2train.com, 2005; 2KGames, 2005; The Sims, 2005). Simulations also involve decision making that engages the affective domain of users.

Of course, not all games work at this level. Many are task-oriented activities that mask language-learning skills in new technology. *Hot Potatoes* (Half-Baked Software, 2005) was designed as an interactive language-learning tool that permits teachers to construct crossword puzzles, jumbled sentences, and interactive multiple-choice activities. *Puzzlemaker* at Discovery Schools.com (2004) offers some of the same options.

Given what we know about Millennials' distain for simple games, the emphasis on using Internet or stand-alone games should be on complexity and challenge, not on drill (Prensky, 2005). When used properly, the new generation of interactive games can provoke rich affective, language-intensive opportunities for ELLs and special needs students.

SYNCHRONOUS AND ASYNCHRONOUS COMMUNICATION

Communication and computing devices have become portable, and in many cases wearable. Computer-mediated communication with portable devices occurs as individuals or groups talk with each other across town or across the country. Temporally concurrent communication is conversational, and is referred to as *synchronous* communication (e.g., cell phones). *Asynchronous* communication is not concurrent and occurs at the convenience of each participant (e.g., e-mail). Synchronous e-learning may utilize cell phones, instant messaging, chat rooms, and webcams while asynchronous e-learning would involve computer-mediated e-mail exchange, text messaging, blogs, and MP3 players. While cell phone use requires listening, processing, and response skills, text messaging, e-mail, and chat room interaction engages students in textual interpretation and text-based response. With the advent of portable communication devices (e.g., cell phones, wireless laptops, PDAs, and Bluetooth), classroom walls have been eliminated. This new dimension of e-learning has been referred to as *m-learning*, or mobile learning. Teaching and learning within the mobile dimension can be synchronous or asynchronous, and can occur either via wireless (WiFi) networks or through a standard modem connection.

When applied to language learning, m-learning is referred to as mobile assisted language learning, or MALL. As a mobile form of CALL, language learning with portable devices incorporates many of the components of traditional CALL—students listen to recordings using MP3 players and they read and write text from e-mail, blogs, and cell-mediated text messaging. On the synchronous end of m-learning, students listen and respond to cell phone calls, and dialogue by means of text in chat rooms and computer-mediated instant messaging.

Synchronous Communication

Cell Phones and Text Messaging. Contemporary cell phones have numerous options. Features include voice and text messaging, point-to-point intercom capabilities, message recording, Internet connectivity, digital photography, and a video display.

Klund and Novak (2001) suggest that the use of word prediction software improves the quality and quantity of written work. A form of predictive software is included in most cell phone operating systems. Cell phone e-mail, called text messaging (e.g., TXTs), is ubiquitous among many digital natives. Real-time messaging occurs through the medium of character selection and input using the phone keypad. Text messaging can also serve as a form of m-learning, as students send and receive messages on the go. The text system used on cells is called *Short Message Service* (SMS). SMS can handle the transmission of up to 160 letters and spaces per message. Text abbreviations such as LOL (laugh out loud) and IML8 (I am late) are commonly used. While whole words and entire sentences can be transmitted as TXTs, the preferred method involves the extensive use of abbreviations. While this may seem counterproductive for second-language instruction, SMS communication offers the option for the use of *predictive text*. This format, embedded in most cell phones as a form of text editor, permits users to begin typing a word. The word stem is identified in the predictive text dictionary, which then replaces the word stem with a whole word. If the word selected is not the word intended the user has the option to select other best-fit words.

Chinnery (2006) describes several projects that have used text messaging in ESL programs. He relates that SMS activities increased the number of new vocabulary words students learned and had the effect of improved test scores. Students also indicated that they preferred to continue using SMS-based lessons. While fewer words were used by SMS users, they were able to communicate more effectively (p. 11). Word prediction and text-to-speech programs for special needs students act as *word coaches* for struggling writers (Lankutis & Kennedy, 2002, p. 3). They relate that students can type in the first few letters of a word and receive a list of word options to choose from.

Instant messaging. Instant messaging (IM), according to Sotillo (2006), has the potential to reduce the affective filter and facilitate interaction among participants. IM uses a client software program that permits real-time communication over the Internet from computer to computer, or from cell phones. Communication can be one-on-one or occur in groups. Commonly used programs include Windows Messenger, AOL Messenger, and MSN Messenger. Cziko and Park (2003) make several IM program recommendations based on the needs of ELLs and the functions of client programs. They suggest that PalkTalk, Yahoo Messenger, and iVisit may offer unique opportunities for teachers who desire to create public or private audio chats for ELLs (p. 14). Messengers are primarily text-based, and permit users to invite others to participate as contacts. Text messages may include emoticons in much the same way as e-mail.

Depending upon which IM program is selected, contacts can send real-time text messages, digital pictures, and video or use voice communication. IM applications include collaborative activities, group discussions, mentoring opportunities, and remote guest speakers (Farmer, 2003). ELLs may use IM to converse with speakers of their home language or with second-language mentors. Participants can discuss interpersonal themes, events, and acquaintances in their home country as well as engage in multimedia exchange activities. Teachers can monitor discussions as well as capture sessions for review and analysis using IM capture tools (Godwin-Jones, 2005).

Chat rooms. As a form of socially interactive instruction, chat rooms may be created through instant messenger programs that support multimedia communication. They may also utilize existing text-based applications called Internet Relay Chats (IRCs) that permit real-time discussions between individuals and groups anywhere in the world (LeLoup & Ponterio, 2003, p.5).

Synchronous chat room forums are hosted by providers such as America on Line (AOL), Yahoo, and Dave's ESL Chat Central. They may be closed to the uninvited, or open to all. For instance, Dave's Café (2006) contains separate chat rooms for different topics such as students, teachers, grammar, and jobs. Participants may join at will. When a room is populated by ELLs of different levels of ability, chats may lag as members who may choose not to participate listen in the background.

The use of chat rooms has become somewhat controversial. Closed chat rooms that do not permit outsiders provide needed security and at the same time function as viable spaces for students to practice literacy skills. Teachers, mentors, or monitors can coordinate discussions and mediate grammar and structural difficulties, and review chat room transcripts. Mynard (2002) summarizes the effects of chat room use on ESL students. Chat rooms promote communication in authentic contexts and active involvement; they permit learner autonomy; and they offer opportunities for participants to practice their skills.

Asynchronous Communication: E-Mail and Blogs

E-mail. E-mail used in second-language instruction precipitates language production, encourages peer-to-peer interaction, and promotes intercultural understanding. It may also decrease anxiety among learners and increase motivation (LeLoup & Ponterio, 2003). Through the use of e-mail, teachers are able to monitor conversations and check student progress. E-mail activities can be structured or unstructured, and include teacher-initiated writing prompts, chain stories, and cloze exercises (Gonglewski, Meloni, & Brant, 2001). Correspondents use graphic *emoticons* or *smileys* (e.g., :-) "smiling"; :-("sad") to add an element of affective communication. They may also use adapted e-mail programs that are picture based rather than text based and web browser speech synthesis capabilities (e-Bility.com, 2006).

Pen-pal exchanges, or tandem writing, have evolved into long-distance e-mail connections called ePals or Keypals. The *ePals Global Network* (2006) touts connections among 6 million students and teachers in 191 countries. An ancillary program called *School Mail* is reported to provide safety and privacy to users. Another benefit, especially for language learners, is School Mail's ability to translate e-mail across several languages.

Blogs. Blogs, short for *weblogs*, had their start as online journals. Since 2003 they have evolved from text-based journals to multimedia websites that incorporate digital photos, video, audio, and hyperlinks. One of the more popular blog hosts—Blogger—offers users free access and has the capability to permit collaborative journaling and peer-review editing (Stiler, 2003).

Blogging can offer English language learners and special needs students a unique platform from which they can actually publish meaningful multimedia autobiographies. Blogger offers a helper tool that links text from a writing program (e.g., Microsoft Word) to a user's blog. Students can add digital photos and video clips of people, places, pets, or families and add hyperlinks that connect their stories to sites of interest. Users can embed map locations into their blog with XML (Extensible Markup Language). This link takes readers to a specified map location. Blogs also offer the potential to integrate m-learning options. Students can add audio content from cell phones at their convenience and discretion.

The applications discussed here are certainly not exhaustive. There are many other forms of emerging technologies and software included in the broad scope of computer-assisted language learning. As practitioners, teachers need to see themselves as early adaptors, yet at the same time engage in a process that evaluates emerging technology, as it may or may not coincide with the best interests of their students.

CHAPTER SUMMARY

This chapter presents an array of literacy strategies and technology support resources and activities that could be used as starting ideas for instructional adaptations. As you have seen in this chapter, the ideas presented are research-based or research-related strategies. All of these suggested literacy and technology activities support the notion that mainstream teachers can use reading and writing as a primary tool for teaching all their learners. In that challenge, technology can certainly provide assistance as not only the process tool for learning but also a tool to manage learning. Teachers can integrate various technology strategies with reading and writing as these two modes of teaching take the center stage for teaching ELLs and SNSs in the mainstream classrooms

REFERENCES

Anderson, V., & Roit, M. (1996). Linking reading comprehension instruction to language development for language minority students. *The Elementary School Journal, 96*, 295–309.

Apple Education. (2002). The impact of technology on student achievement. Cupertino, CA: Apple Computer, Inc. Retrieved March 16, 2006, from http://www.apple.com/education/research/.

Arrison, S. (2002). What digital divide? Pacific Research Institute, CNet News.com. Retrieved March 16, 2006, from http://www.pacificresearch.org/press/opd/2002/opd_02-03-14sa.html.

August, D., & Hakuta, K. (1997). *Improving schooling for language-minority children.* Washington DC: National Academy Press.

Baker, C. (1996). *Foundations of bilingual education and bilingualism.* Philadelphia, PA: Multilingual Matters Ltd.

Bax, S. (2003). CALL-past, present and future. *System, 21*, 13–28.

Behrmann, M. (1998). Assistive technology for young children in special education. In C. Dede (Ed.), *Learning with technology* (pp. 73–93). Alexandria, VA: ASCD.

Bialystok, E. (2002). Acquisition of literacy in bilingual children: A framework for research. *Language Learning, 52*, 159–199.

Billmeyer, R., & Barton, M. (1998). *Teaching reading in the content areas.* Aurora,CO: McREL.

Blair-Larsen, S., & Williams, K. (Eds.). (1999). *The balanced reading program: Helping all students achieve success.* Newark, DE: International Reading Association.

Blankenship, T., Ayers, K., & Langone, J. (2005). Effects of computer-based cognitive mapping on reading comprehension for students with emotional behavior disorders. *Journal of Special Education Technology, 20*(2), 15–23.

Braddock, D., Rizzolo, M., Thompson, M., & Bell, R. (2004). Emerging technologies and cognitive disabilities. *Journal of Special Education Technology, 19*(4).

Bridwell, L. (1980). Revising strategies in twelfth grade students' transactional writing. *Research in the Teaching of English, 14*, 197–222.

Brooks-Young, S. (2005). Video streaming: Harnessing a unique capability of technology. Today's school. Retrieved March 15, 2006, from http://www.peterli.com/archive/ts/912.shtm.

Bryant, J., Sanders-Jackson, A., & Smallwood, A. (2006). IMing, text messaging and adolescent social networks. *Journal of Computer-Mediated Communication, 11*(2), article 10. Retrieved March 22, 2006, from http://www.jcmc.indiana.edu/vol11/issue2/bryant.html.

Bryant, P. E., & Goswami, U. (1987). Phonological awareness and learning to read. In J. R.

Beech & A. M. Colley (Eds.), *Cognitive approaches to reading.* New York: Wiley.

Chamot, A. (1995). Implementing the cognitive academic language learning approach:

CALLA in Arlington, Virginia. *The Bilingual Research Journal, 19*(3 & 4), 379–394.

Chamot, A., & O'Malley, J. M. (1996). The cognitive academic language learning approach: A model for linguistically diverse classroom. *The Elementary School Journal, 96*, 259–273.

Chow, P. (2001). The dual language showcase. Retrieved March 15, 2006, from http://thornwood.peelschools.org/Dual/.

Chun, D., & Plass, J. (1996). Effects of multimedia annotations on vocabulary acquisition. *Modern Language Journal, 80*, 183–198.

Clip Art for L2 Instruction. (2003). Retrieved March 16, 2006, from http://tell.fll.purdue.edu/JapanProj//FLClipart/.

Combs, M. (2002). *Readers and writers in primary grades: A balanced and integrated approach.* Upper Saddle River, NJ: Merrill Prentice Hall

Cooper, D. (2003). *Literacy: Helping children construct meaning.* Boston, MA: Houghton Mifflin Company.

Cummins, J. (1979). Linguistic interdependence and the educational development of bilingual children. *Review of Educational Research, 49*, 222–251.

Cummins, J. (2001). *Negotiating identities: Education for empowerment in a diverse society.* Los Angeles, CA: California Association for Bilingual Education.

Cziko, G., & Park, S. (2003). Internet audio communication for second language learning: A comparative review of six programs. *Language, Learning and Technology , 7*(1), 15–27.

Dahl, K. L., & Farnan, N. (1998). *Children's writing: Perspective from research.* Newark, DE: International Reading Association.

Dave's Café. (2006). Retrieved March 22, 2006, from http://www.eslcafe.com/.

Diary Project. (2003). Retrieved March 15, 2006, from http://www.diaryproject.com/.

Digital Media. (2005). Retrieved March 15, 2005, from http://www.digitalcurriculum.com/.

Discovery School Clip Art Gallery. (2005). Retrieved March 16, 2006, from http://school.discovery.com/clipart/.

Discovery Schools.com. (2004). Puzzlemaker. Retrieved March 16, 2006, from http://puzzlemaker.school.discovery.com/.

Durgunoglu, A. Y., Nagy, W.E., & Hancin-Batt, B. J. (1993). Cross-language transfer of phonological awareness. *Journal of Educational Psychology, 85*, 453–465.

Dyson, A. H. (1983). The role of oral language in early writing processes. *Research in the Teaching of English, 17*, 1–30.

Dyson, A. H. (1992). Whistle for Willie, lost puppies and cartoon dogs: The sociocultural dimensions of young children's composing. *Journal of Reading Behavior, 24*, 433–461.

e-Bility.com. (2006). Software for people with disabilities. Retrieved April 18, 2006, from http://e-bility.com/links/software.php.

Echevarria, J., Vogt, M., & Short, D. J. (2000). *Making content comprehensible for English language learners.* Needham Heights, MA: Allyn & Bacon.

Edelsky, C. (1982). Writing in a bilingual program: The relation of L1 and L2 texts. *TESOL Quarterly, 16*(2), 211–228.

Ehri, L. & Nunes S. (2002). The role of phonemic awareness in learning to read. In A. Farstrup & S. J. Samuels (Eds.), *What research has to say about reading instruction* (pp. 110–139). Newark, DE: International Reading Association.

Emig, J. (1971). *The composing process of twelfth graders.* Urbana, IL: National Council of Teachers of English.

ePals Global Network. (2006). Retrieved March 18, 2006, from http://www.epals.com/.

Farmer, R. (2003). Instant messaging—collaborative tool or educator's nightmare? *NAWeb 2003.* Retrieved March 22, 2006, from http://www.unb.ca/naweb/proceedings/2003/PaperFarmer.html.

Farmer, R. (2005). Instant messaging: IM Online! *RU? EDUCAUSE Review, 40*(6), 48–67.

Flower, L., & Hayes, J. (1977). Problem-solving strategies and the writing process. *College English, 39*, 449–461.

Flower, L., & Hayes, J. (1980). The cognition of discovery: Defining a rhetorical problem. *College Composition and Communication, 31*, 21–32.

Fox, S., & Madden, M. (2005). Generations online. Pew Internet and American Life Project, Data Memo.

Games2train.com. (2005). Retrieved March 16, 2006, from http://www.socialimpactgames.com/.

Garcia. E. (1999). *Student cultural diversity: Understanding and meeting the challenge.* Boston, MA: Houghton Mifflin Company.

Garcia, G., & Beltran, D. (Eds.). (2003). *Reaching the highest level of English literacy.* International Reading Association.

Godwin-Jones, B. (2005). Emerging technologies: Messaging, gaming, peer-to-peer sharing: language learning strategies and tools for the millennial generation. *Language Learning and Technology, 9*(1), 17–22.

Gonglewski, M., Meloni, C., & Brant, J. (2001). Using e-mail in foreign language instruction: Rationale and suggestions. *The Internet TESL Journal, 7*(3). Retrieved March 17, 2006, from http://iteslj.org/Techniques/Meloni-Email.html.

Goodman, K., Goodman, Y., & Flores, B. (1979). *Reading in the bilingual classroom: Literacy and biliteracy.* Rosslyn, VA: National Clearinghouse for Bilingual Education.

Google Images. (2006). Retrieved March 16, 2006, from http://images.google.com/.

Graves, D. H. (1975). An examination of the writing processes of seven-year old children. *Research in the Teaching of English, 9*, 227–241.

Graves, D. H. (1979). A six-year-old's writing process: The first half of first grade. *Language Arts, 56*, 829–835.

Gunning, T. (2005). *Creating literacy instruction for all students.* Boston, MA: Pearson Education , Inc.

Half-Baked Software. (2005). Hot potatoes (Version 6.0)@Computer software:. Retrieved March 16, 2006, from http://web.uvic.ca/hrd/hotpot/.

Hall, T., & Strangman, N. (2002). Graphic organizers. Wakefield, MA: National Center on Accessing the General Curriculum. Retrieved March 16, 2006, from http://www.cast.org/publications/ncac/ncac_go.html.

Hawking, S. (2001). *Computer resources for people with disabilities.* Petaluma, CA: Alliance for Technology Access.

Honey, M., Culp, K., & Carrigg, F. (1999). *Perspectives on technology and education research: Lesson from the past and present.* Washington, DC: U.S. Department of Education, the Secretary's Conference on Educational Technology.

Howe, N., & Strauss, W. (2000). *Millenials rising: The next great generation.* New York: Vintage Books.

Hughey, J. B., & Slack, C. (2001). *Teaching children to write: Theory into practice.* Columbus, OH: Merrill Prentice Hall.

Inspiration Software. (2003). Inspiration/Kidspiration. [Computer software]. Beaverton, OR: Inspiration Software, Inc.

Kalyanpur, M., & Kirmani, M. (2005). Diversity and technology: Classroom implications and the digital divide. *Journal of Special Education Technology, 20*(4), 9–17.

Kaye. (2000). *Computer and Internet use among people with disabilities. Disability statistics report.* Washington, DC: U.S. Department of Education, National Institute on Disability and Rehabilitation Research.

Kimble, C. (1999). The impact of technology on learning: Making sense of the research. Aurora, CO: Mid-continent Regional Educational Laboratory Brief. Retrieved March 16, 2006, from http://www.mcrel.org/ PDFConversion/PolicyBriefs/PB_ImpactTechnology.html.

Klund, J., & Novak, M. (2001). If word prediction can help, which program do you choose? Paper presented at the 1995 Closing the Gap Conference, Minneapolis, MN.

Lalas, J., Solomon, M,. Franklin, M. Unterreiner, A., Langford, S., & Stiler, G. (2005). A metacognitive professional development model for academic literacy. Improving Teacher Quality State (CA) Grants Program. Unpublished proposal.

Lalas, J., Solomon, M., & Stiler, G. (March, 2005). Academic literacy development: Technology driven reading and writing connection. Paper presented at the California Association for Bilingual Education conference, San Jose, CA.

Langer, J. (1986). *Children reading and writing: Structures and strategies.* Norwood, NJ: Ablex. Language Teaching Clip Art. (n.d.). Retrieved March 16, 2006, from http://web.uvic.ca/hcmc/clipart/.

Lankutis, T., & Kennedy, K. (2002, March 1). Assistive technology and the multiage classroom. *Technology & Learning,* 1–5.

LeLoup, J., & Ponterio, R. (2003). Second language acquisition and technology: A review of the research. Retrieved March 15, 2006, from http://www.cal.org/resources/digest/031lecoup.html.

Lenhart, A., Madden, M., & Hitlin, P. (2005). *Teens and technology: Youth are leading the transition to a fully wired and mobile nation.* Washington, DC: Pew Internet & American Life Project.

Manzo, A., Manzo, U., & Thomas, M. (2005). *I read it, but I don't get it: Comprehension strategies for adolescent readers.* John Wiley & Sons, Inc.

Mechling, L. (2005). The effect of instructor-created video programs to teach students with disabilities: A literature review. *Journal of Special Education Technology, 20*(2), 25–36.

Mechling, L., Ghast, D., & Langone, J. (2002). Computer-based video instruction to teach persons with moderate intellectual disabilities to read grocery aisle signs and locate items. *Journal of Special Education Technology, 35*(4), 224–240.

Minami, M., & Kennedy, B. (Eds.). (1998). *Language issues in literacy and bilingual/multicultural education.* Cambridge, MA: Harvard Educational Review.

Montague, N. (1995) The process oriented approach to teaching writing to second language learners. *New York State Association for Bilingual Education Journal, 10,* 13–24.

Murray, D. H. (1982). *Learning by teaching.* Montclair, NJ: Boyton/Cook.

O'Malley, M., & Chamot, A. (1990). *Learning strategies in second language acquisition.* Cambridge: Cambridge University Press.

Perfetti, C. A., Beck, I., Bell, L. C., & Hughes, C. (1988). Phonemic knowledge and learning to read are reciprocal: A longitudinal study of first grade children. In K. E. Stanovich (Ed.), *Children's reading and the development of phonological awareness* (pp. 39–75). Detroit, MI: Wayne University Press.

Pics4Learning. (2002). Retrieved March 16, 2006, from http://pics.tech4learning.com/.

Picture Dictionary. (2004). Retrieved March 16, 2006, from http://www.enchantedlearning.com/Home.html.

Powermedia. (2006). Retrieved March 15, 2006, from http://www.powermediaplus.com/.

Prensky, M. (2001). Digital natives, digital immigrants. *On the Horizon, 9*(5). Retrieved March 16, 2006, from http://www.marcprensky.com/writing/Prensky%20-%20Digital%20Natives,%20Digital%20 Immigrants%20-%20Part1.pdf.

Prensky, M. (2005). In educational games, complexity matters. *Educational Technology, 45*(4). Retrieved March 16, 2005, from http://www.marcprensky.com/writing/Prensky-Complexity_Matters.pdf.

Quinn, C. (March, 2000). M-learning: Mobile, wireless, in-your-pocket learning. *LiNE*

Zine: Learning in the New Economy. *Retrieved March 17, 2006, from http://www.linezine.com/2.1/features/ cqmmwiyp.htm.*

Raimes, A. (1991). Out of the woods: Emerging traditions in the teaching of writing. *TESOL Quarterly, 25,* 279–304.

Raines, C. (2003). *Connecting generations: The sourcebook.* Mississauga, Ontario: Crisp Learning.

Readence, J., Bean, T., & Baldwin, R. (2000). *Content area literacy: An integrated approach.* Dubuque, IA: Kendall/Hunt Publishing Company.

Rose, D., & Meyer, A. (2000). The future is in the margins: The role of technology and disability in educational reform. Washington, DC: U.S. Department of Education, Office of Special Education Technology.

Reyes, M. (1992). Challenging venerable assumptions. *Harvard Educational Review, 62*(4), 427–446.

Reyes, M., Lalibery, E., & Orbansky, J. (1993). Emerging biliteracy and cross-cultural sensitivity in a language arts classroom. *Language Arts, 70,* 659–668.

Ruddell, M. (2005). *Teaching content reading and writing.* Denver, MA: John Wiley & Sons.

Short, D. (1991, Fall). Integrating language and content instruction: Strategies and techniques, NCELA Program Information Guide Series, Number 7, p. 797.

Snow, C., Burns, M., & Griffin, P. (1998). *Preventing reading difficulties in young children.* Washington DC: National Academy Press.

Spiro, R., Bruce, B., & Brewer, W. (1980). *Theoretical issues in reading comprehension.* Hillsdale, NJ: Lawrence Erlbaum Associates.

Svedkauskaite, A., & Reza-Hernandez, L. (2003). Critical issue: Using technology to support limited-English-proficient (LEP) students' learning experiences. Naperville, IL: North Central Regional Educational Laboratory. Retrieved March 16, 2006, from http://www.ncrel.org/sdrs/areas/issues/methods/technlgy/te900.htm.

Tapscott. (1999). *Growing up digital: The rise of the net generation.* New York: McGraw-Hill.

Tarlow, M., & Tarlow, P. (2002). *Digital aboriginal: The direction of business now: Instinctive, nomadic, and ever-changing.* Lebanon, IN Warner Business Books.

The Jason Project. (2005). Retrieved March 15, 2006, from http://www.jasonproject.org/.

The Sims. (2005). [Computer software]. Redwood City, CA: Electronic Arts Inc.

Thinkport. (2006). Online field trips. Maryland Public Television and Johns Hopkins University Center for Technology in Education. Retrieved March 22, 2006, from http://www.thinkport.org/about.tp.

Tompkins, G. E. (2006). *Literacy for the 21st century.* Columbus, OH: Merrill/Prentice Hall.

Tompkins, G. (2007). *Literacy for the 21st century: Teaching reading and writing in prekindergarten through grade 4.* Upper Saddle River: NJ: Merrill/Prentice Hall.

Tovani, C. (2000). *I read it, but I don't get it.* Portland, MA: Stenhouse Publishers.

2KGames. (2005). *Civilization III.* [Computer software]. New York: 2KGames.

UnitedStreaming. (2005). Retrieved March 15, 2006, from http://school.discovery.com/.

Unrau, N. (2004). *Content area reading and writing.* Upper Saddle River, NJ: Pearson Education.

U.S. Department of Commerce. (2002). A nation online: How Americans are expanding their use of the Internet. Washington, DC:

U.S. Department of Commerce. (2004). A nation online: How Americans are expanding their use of the Internet. National Telecommunications and Information Administration. Retrieved March 16, 2006, from http://www.ntia.doc.gov/reports/anol/index.html.

Utah Education Network. (2005). Retrieved March 15, 2006, from http://www.uen.org/utahlink/tours/ fieldtrips2.htm.

Virtual Visits. (2004). Retrieved March 15, 2006, from http://alri.org/visits/vv.html.

Vygotsky, L. S. (1978). *Mind in society: The development of higher psychological processes.* Cambridge, MA: Harvard University Press.

Wagner, R. K., Torgesen, J. K., & Rashotte, C. A. (1994). Development of reading-related phonological processing ability: New evidence of bidirectional causality from a latent variable longitudinal study. *Developmental Psychology, 30,* 73–87.

Wallace, S. (2004).Effective instructional strategies for English language learners in mainstream classrooms. *New Horizons for Learning Online Journal, 12*(1). Retrieved March 17, 2006, from http://www.newhorizons.org/spneeds/ell/wallace.htm#a.

WebQuests. (2000). Retrieved March 16, 2006, http://www.biopoint.com/.

WebQuest.org. (2006). Retrieved March 16, 2006, from http://webquest.org/.

Wiggleworks. (2006). [Computer software]. Retrieved March 15, 2006, from http://teacher.scholastic.com/products/wiggleworks/index.htm.

Williams, K., & Gomez, L. (2001). Presumptive literacies in technology-integrated science curriculum. Retrieved March 16, 2006, from http://newmedia.colorado.edu/cscl/262.

Wong-Filmore, L., & Valadez, C. (1986). Teaching bilingual learners. In M.C. Wittrock (Ed.), *Handbook of research on teaching* (pp. 648–685). New York: Macmillan.

CHAPTER

The Conclusion: Making and Sustaining
Instructional Adaptation for Educational Justice

This book has made the case for mainstream teachers making instructional adaptations as part of their instructional repertoire. We believe that the effort of making special accommodations to provide *all* students access to academic content curriculum and instruction is a good example of creating an educationally just learning environment. However, differentiating instruction for ELLs and SNSs through various instructional adaptations cannot take place simply. As you have gathered from the previous chapters of this book, it takes knowledge, experience, disposition, a sense of social justice, an ethic of caring, and self-reflection on the part of the teacher to engage in undertakings that will advance and sustain the notion of educational justice for equity solution in the classroom for all students, including English language and special needs learners.

In the context of making instructional adaptations for the target learners, we recommend in this book that teachers become active, life-long learners to empower themselves with research-based theories and "best practices" in addressing the various instructional challenges they face. Teachers must also become responsive to teaching special learners by engaging in "critical pedagogy" to meet the unique needs of these learners. We define "critical pedagogy" basically as the "art of reflective teaching that involves providing opportunities and experiences for students to raise their levels of social/political consciousness as well as their personal/community/global awareness for potential transformation and social action" (Lalas & Horton, 2002). "If teachers are to prepare an ever more diverse group of students for much more challenging work . . . they will need substantially more knowledge and radically different skills than most now have and most schools of education now develop" (Bransford, Brown, & Cocking, 1999, p. 178).

We would like to highlight in our conclusion that one of this book's underlying implications is that through continuous **teacher learning,** or commonly understood as professional development, teachers not only can experience the renewal of their teaching identity and passion but also upgrade and reframe the knowledge, skills, abilities, and disposition that are essential in making positive influences in the lives of their English language and special needs learners. The other important implication of the book is the significant role that **reflection,** an intentional, deliberative, and conscious process, plays in providing the personal, psychological, social, and cultural awareness and the metacognitive process that drives the interaction of students, teachers, and contexts in the mainstream classroom.

ONGOING TEACHER LEARNING IS VITAL

In helping the English language and special needs learners in the mainstream classroom, the key factor in the teacher learning process is the acceptance of the need for change in the instructional paradigm by allowing adaptations for ELLs and SNSs. There is no doubt that teachers have to re-think their assumptions about the different cultural and learning characteristics of their students and enhance their understanding and knowledge of diversity. According to Darling-Hammond and Baratz-Snowden (2005), in order to facilitate learning in a democratic society, beginning teachers must understand how children learn and develop in social contexts, must know the subject matter they will teach, must understand how to organize school curriculum in light of what the students need, and must have the teaching skill that engages learners to access the curriculum.

Teacher learning as an ongoing process is vital in advancing and sustaining teacher development in the areas of understanding children and learning, pedagogy and assessment, and subject-matter content knowledge. Currently, professional development literature presents several perspectives about teacher learning (Darling-Hammond & Baratz-Snowden, 2005; Darling-Hammond & Sykes, 1999). One perspective represents the traditional, externally driven professional development process in which consultants and specialists are hired to share some new information with teachers. The other perspective supports the idea of a teacher becoming the self-directed learner by developing personal knowledge and skills to meet the demands of the classroom through reflection. As an independent artisan "the individual teacher serves as arbiter of new ideas, adopting or adapting some, rejecting others . . . Learning is largely self-selected and self-directed" (Sykes, 1999, p. 157). Here the teacher freely chooses what is best for him or her and may even modify and change practice to transform student learning. In another perspective on teacher learning, teachers are viewed as social beings who interact with their environment constantly, where learning is structured within the cultural and organizational context of the school and teacher collaboration is the core feature.

Whatever perspective is taken, we all understand and embrace the reality that preservice and inservice teachers are active and life-long learners. More importantly, as part of their ongoing teacher learning, beginning teachers and experienced teachers must engage in conversations and pursuits of action related to educational justice agenda, such as understanding oneself in relation to others, appreciating diversity and promoting equity, recognizing inequalities and attempting to diminish them, encouraging equitable participation and adequate allocation of resources, creating a caring and culturally responsive learning environment, working together as a learning community, facilitating classroom inquiry as well as critical thinking and reflection, and using varied forms of assessment as an equity solution (Gordon, Lalas, & McDermott, 2006).

Teachers in today's complex and diverse classrooms have the opportunity and challenge to navigate children and young adults' lives by engaging in an ongoing search, examination, application, evaluation, and reflection of theory and practice that intensifies the acquisition of knowledge and development of disposition of all learners in a democratic and educationally just society.

TEACHER REFLECTION: VITAL TOOL FOR MAKING AND SUSTAINING ADAPTATIONS

After working with school districts in New York for implementing schoolwide instructional change, Elmore and Burney (1999) asserted that successful professional development "focuses on concrete classroom applications of general ideas; it exposes teachers to actual practice rather than to descriptions of practice; it offers opportunities for observation, critique, and reflection" (p. 263). Richardson (1994) proposed a collaborative and purposeful inquiry-based professional development with reflection as the core learning process. Apparently, reflection appears to be a vital tool for facilitating professional development or teacher learning in today's classrooms. It helps teachers deal with different kinds of uncertainties involved in working with diverse students in the classroom in a deliberative and intentional manner. It also engages teachers to function with self-awareness, self-inquiry, and self-reflection (Cooper & Larrivee, 2006).

Reflection helps teachers to look at instructional dilemmas critically and think about how best they can manage teaching all learners, including the English language and special needs learners. Reflection becomes the process for teachers "to see student learning; to discern, differentiate, and describe the elements of learning, to analyze the learning and to respond . . ." (Rodgers, 2002, p. 231). According to Schon (1983), reflection goes beyond the traditional ways of analysis and problem solving. It goes further than what one sees on the surface and calls for mindfulness and looking at the details of the moments considered. It is the process of "knowing in action, which reaches beyond what we can say we know to what we know but cannot say . . . the process that underlies knowing in action is reflecting-in-action or reflecting-in-practice or . . . thinking on your feet" (Tremmel, 1993; Schon, 1983, p. 54).

Rodgers (2002) explains that there are two specific goals or advantages for teachers in doing reflection:

> The first is to develop their capacity to observe skillfully and to think critically about students and their learning so they learn to consider what this tells them about teaching the subject matter and the context in which all of these interact. The second goal is for them to begin to take intelligent action based on the understanding that emerges. (pp. 231–232)

This view depicts reflection as an active teacher learning process that can be used by individual teachers or by a team of teachers in order to bring the needed changes in their pedagogy and support the learning of special learners. Rodgers (2002) conceptualizes the framework of reflection in four different learning phases, as described in Figure 5.1.

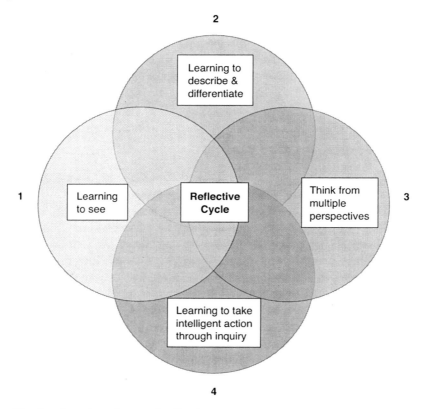

Figure 5.1   The four learning phases of reflection.

LEARNING TO SEE

Teacher reflection begins with learning to see the details of their teaching and student learning, which is well described by the term "presence in experience." In this first step teachers are asked to come to a state of mind that focuses on the ability "to be present to students' learning and able to respond with the best possible next instructional move . . . the more a teacher is present, the more she can perceive, the more she perceives, the greater the potential for an intelligent response" (Rodgers, 2002, p. 234). Mainstream teachers learn to be present and attentive to all aspects of their teaching and learning that take place for all students, including ELLs and SNSs, in their classrooms. They "pay attention right here, right now, and invest in the present moment with full awareness and concentration" (Tremmel, 1993, p. 433) so they can make immediate adjustments as classroom events occur. Observing student responses and making the necessary adjustments while in the process of teaching can also be referred to as "reflection-in-action" (Schon, 1987).

In this initial step, teachers learn to really "see" what's going on for their students and about their teaching. It aims to help them look at the learning dilemmas of students before teaching, while teaching, and after teaching. This also provides an excellent opportunity for teachers to individually look into their personal beliefs, attitudes, abilities, and dispositions about working with diverse students.

LEARNING TO DESCRIBE AND DIFFERENTIATE

In the next phase, teachers collaborate with other colleagues in looking at the different instructional dilemmas they face by describing, interpreting, and differentiating the teaching and learning events through open conversations. They bring various selected "moments" of their teaching and share them with other colleagues. The purpose of this sharing is "to dig up as many details as possible, from as many different angles possible so that one is not limited to the sum of one's own perceptions" (Rodgers, 2002, p. 238). They also get feedback from students about the teaching moment selected to understand the difficulties they have experienced. These detailed descriptions help teachers to interpret the event from multiple points of view.

In this phase of the reflection process, the teachers dialogue with colleagues about the identified teaching and learning dilemmas for ELLs and SNSs. This dialogue, often called "collaborative critical dialogue," is between the teacher and colleagues when they question one another about what was taught and learned and what difficulties they experienced. "In an atmosphere of trust, well-crafted questions allow participants to reveal their insights, understandings, and thought processes" (Costa & Kallick, 2000, p. 3). The dialogue continues until resolutions for the teaching dilemmas are determined, shared, and discussed. Teachers learn skills in describing, interpreting, and analyzing classroom events and further verify their analytical understanding by asking students to give feedback.

LEARNING TO THINK CRITICALLY FROM MULTIPLE VIEWS

In this learning phase, teachers generate different explanations about a selected teaching event or episode with colleagues. "Although it comes after description, there is often a dialectical relationship between the two. During the analysis it is sometimes necessary to return to the descriptive phase and seek more data, which in turn may point toward different analyses" (Rodgers, 2002, p. 244). In this phase, teachers' assumptions, prior knowledge, and beliefs are unearthed, making this a very essential part of reflection. The purpose is to see how personal theories and assumptions about student learning influence their teaching. In the case of teaching the English language and special needs learners, teachers will discover their personal beliefs, attitudes, and understanding of issues related to working with these special learners. Teachers' prior and existing knowledge, abilities, and views become the content of discussion and analysis. By describing and analyzing a selected teaching event for their special learners, teachers are given the opportunity not only to reorganize and reconstruct their experiences but also to think about an intelligent, appropriate, and relevant future action (Rodgers, 2002).

This phase provides the opportunity to bring some instructional and curricular solutions to the teaching and learning problems related to the instruction of ELLs and SNSs. Teachers learn new techniques to remediate the weaknesses or enrich the strengths identified in the teaching dilemmas they continually face with these special students. Their focus is to learn to make appropriate and relevant instructional adaptations to facilitate access to grade-level subject-matter academic content. They learn to make adaptations by paying attention to related academic content standards, learning goals, teachers' instructional strategies, student activities, and assessment before, during, and after instruction.

LEARNING TO TAKE INTELLIGENT ACTION THROUGH INQUIRY

"Experimentation is the final as well as the initial phase of the reflective cycle . . . at some point the ideas of action that teachers settle on must be tested in action . . ." (Rodgers, 2002, p. 249). This inquiry is done mainly for improving their teaching and student learning by gathering convincing evidence through a simple research process. Teachers select instructional adaptation strategies with specific goals of inquiry in mind and see how they impact student learning by collecting various evidence. Such an inquiry is called *action research,* which "is a disciplined process of inquiry conducted by and for those taking the action. The primary reason for engaging in action research is to assist the 'actor' in improving and/or refining his/her actions" (Sagor, 2000, p. 4).

Mainstream teachers can analyze the effectiveness of instructional adaptations they make for ELLs and SNSs using the action research process. In fact, action research serves as key to improving teaching. Calhoun (1994) lists various definitions of action research that highlight the importance of improving teaching:

> Action research is a process by which practitioners attempt to study their problems scientifically in order to guide, correct, and evaluate their decisions and actions. Thus action research in education is study conducted by colleagues in a school setting of the results of their activities to improve instruction. Action research is a fancy way of saying, Let's study what's happening at our school and decide how to make it a better place. (p. 20)

CHAPTER SUMMARY

As you have learned from this concluding chapter, the two areas within which all teachers must be striving for optimum engagement as part of their ongoing professional growth are **teacher learning** and **teacher reflection.** We believe that all teachers will continue to improve their delivery of instruction and be effective in working with all students, including English language and special needs learners, by becoming life-long learners and reflective educators. The teacher learning aspect of a teacher's professional growth provides ongoing opportunities for him or her to acquire and develop new beliefs, attitudes, abilities, theories, research-based approaches, and effective instructional practices in working with *all* students, especially in designing and implementing adaptation strategies for the English language and special needs learners. School leadership must take the responsibility to provide a variety of learning opportunities for teachers. Teachers should be supported to take the necessary steps to create appropriate and relevant adaptation strategies, not only as a set of specialized teaching skills for the ELLs and SNSs but as part of their regular teaching repertoire for *all* students in today's diverse schools.

Finally, we believe that deliberative and intentional teaching only occurs when teachers are engaged in reflective practice. Making instructional adaptation as an equity solution for special learners only happens when teachers are **reflective** or consciously involved in thinking about the effectiveness of any teaching episode, the connections between theoretical principles and classroom practice in their own teaching, the moral and ethical implications of their instructional decisions, and the influence of their own personal beliefs and values on students and their learning.

REFERENCES

Bransford, J., Brown, A., & Cocking .(Eds.). (1999). *How people learn: Brain, mind, experience, and school.* New York: National Academy Press.

Calhoun, E. (1994). *How to use action research in the self-renewing school.* Alexandria, VA: Association for Supervision and Curriculum Development.

Cooper & Larrivee. (2006). *An educator's guide to teacher reflection.* New York: Houghton Mifflin Company.

Costa, A. & Kallick, B. (2000). Getting into the habit of reflection. *Educational Leadership, 57* (7).

Darling-Hammond, L., & Baratz-Snowden, J. (2005). *A good teacher in every classroom.* San Francisco, CA: Jossey-Bass.

Darling-Hammond, L., & Sykes, G. (Eds.). (1999). *Teaching as the learning profession: Handbook of policy and practice.* San Francisco, CA: Jossey-Bass.

Elmore, R. F., & Burney, D. (1999). Staff development and instructional improvement. In L. Darling-Hammond & G. Sykes (Eds.), *Teaching as the learning profession: Handbook of policy and practice.* San Francisco, CA: Jossey-Bass Inc.

Gordon, R., Lalas, J., & McDermott, J. C. (2006). *Omni-Education: A teaching and learning framework for social justice in urban classrooms.* Dubuque, IA: Kendall/Hunt Publishing Company.

Lalas, J., & Horton, E. (2002). *Demonstrations: A handbook of balanced literacy ideas and lessons.* Boston, MA: Pearson Custom Publishing.

Richardson, V. (1994). The consideration of teacher's beliefs. In V. Richardson (Ed.), *Teacher change and the staff development process: A case in reading instruction.* New York: Teachers College.

Rodgers, C. R. (2002). Voices inside schools. *Harvard Educational Review, 72* (2).

Sagor, R. (2000). *Guiding school improvement with action research.* Alexandria, VA: Association for Supervision and Curriculum Development.

Schon, D.A. (1983).

Schon, D. A. (1987) *Educating the reflective practitioner.* San Francisco, CA: Jossey-Bass Inc.

Sykes, G. (1999). Teacher and student learning: Strengthening their connection. In L. Darling-Hammond and G. Sykes (Eds.), *Teaching as the learning profession: Handbook of policy and practice.* San Francisco, CA: Jossey-Bass Inc.

Tremmel, R. (1993). Zen and the art of reflective practice in teacher education. *Harvard Educational Review, 63*(4).